A Story That Needs To Be Told

By

Fr. Owen Lally, Passionist

A Legacy of Faith

Our life story is never completed until all of the chapters are in. Some stories have suspense and surprise endings; this one has a lot of twists, turns and wonderful surprises. There are storms at sea, a contract on my life, heavenly visitations, some spiritual warfare and a beautiful deathbed revelation with Fr. Justin. The central and primary protagonist is the Messiah, Jesus, and not I, the witness. I am not a brilliant scholar, so my style is primarily evangelical. It is simply story telling. I enjoyed writing this book.

Fr. Owen, C.P.

Dedicated to the
Glorified Wounds of Jesus
And the Immaculate Heart of Mary.

Table of Contents

Phase One:

Introduction

The Philippine Chapter of my Life

Phase Two:

Scranton

Around the World in 28 Days

Phase Three:

Spiritual Growth

The Stroke

Epilogue
Acknowledgements
Appendix

Phase One

Introduction

I was selling insurance for the N.Y. Life on Long Island and customers very often shared their lives deeply with me. Some needed absolution and I began to desire to give them God's forgiveness. It was the beginning of my vocation to the priesthood. I had never even been an altar boy.

****

One day when I was still attending St. Francis College in Brooklyn, N.Y. I received a piece of bulk mail from the Christopher Movement saying, "Young men, you can change the world. It is better to light one candle than to curse the darkness. Become a politician, a playwright, a teacher, a journalist or something that will influence people's thinking. It will change the world. You only have one life."

This was an anointed piece of mail for me. It changed the direction of my life. I changed my major from business to education. I signed up for the re-tooling program that was being encouraged by the board of education of New York City. In a year and a half I had an M.A. from N.Y.U. in

Elementary Education. I also had a clearer idea of what God was calling me to be. Here is how it happened.

I was "student teaching" at P.S. 125 in Harlem. I was bringing the children back from release time at Corpus Christi parish near Columbia University. We were on the stairwell waiting for another class to pass by. Suddenly I felt a beautiful anointing come over me. I saw in the face of Wilomena, a 10-year-old black girl, all the children of the world. It was luminous. It felt like I was falling in love with the kids of the whole global village. I did not know what it meant until a week later.

I was in my family's home in Queens Village. I was alone. I had just put a piece of bread in the toaster and just in the moment that it took to become toast I knew what was happening to me. God was calling me to be priest.

How could this be? I was a weekend warrior in the U.S. Navy Air Reserves. I had received orders to go on active duty in the Korean conflict. I went immediately to visit my spiritual director Fr. Cosmas Shaughnessy C.P. at the Retreat House in Jamaica. What to do? He told me to get out of the Navy right away, to change my draft status and go immediately to our Prep Seminary in Dunkirk, NY.

I found myself at age 23 back in high school studying Latin. I felt that this where the Spirit led me.

Six years of philosophy and theology retooled me for something far more exciting than the sixth grade classrooms of the school system of New York.

The key person in my spiritual formation was my mother, Irene. She was a great lady and the entire story that follows is her story. The moment that I remember about my mother most vividly was her saying the Stations of the Cross after the morning mass in our Lady of Lourdes Chapel. She invited me to pray with her, station by station. I remember her stopping and sometimes sobbing. It was about my father I think. They had four children and he drank. There was never enough money to meet our needs. We had become poor. Very poor.

In the early days of their marriage there was plenty of money but the depression blew it all away. My father was vice president of an import-export company but when he lost his job all hope seemed to vanish. We lost the house, the car, and the maid that helped my Mom. Irene got a job selling coats at Goodwin's Department store in Jamaica. With the money she earned, she kept food on the table and a roof over our heads.

We moved into a rented dwelling in a poor neighborhood on the other side of the tracks. I really hated the poverty. The walk to school now was very long. I walked through the warehouse and factory section of Queens Village. I really missed my old friends and the familiar old neighborhood.

Church was a place of refuge and of strength for Irene. I learned where to find my help, also.

One deep impression stays with me. I was fooling around with one of my young pals and was unaware of my irreverence in the house of God. Irene let me have it. She made me apologize to God and I had to kneel at the Blessed Mother's altar for a good long while. I asked God for His forgiveness for my bad behavior. It took a while before I felt peace with God again and especially with Irene. It was a lesson I have never forgotten.

Thanks Mom!

Most Irish Catholic mothers I think would like to have a son a priest. How happy Irene was when Bishop O'Gara on my ordination day gave her a brooch as a symbol for the Mother of priest. I think God blessed her with a vocation in the family because of her heroic virtue. For fifteen years, every night she came home from work, exhausted. I greeted her when I could at the Q 36 bus stop at 212th street and Jamaica Avenue. The love we had for each other was very deep but unspoken.

Mom, Dad and me on Ordination Day

Finally, the time for my mission departure arrived. It was really like a death. We were aware we might never see each other again. All the unspoken words of years came surging forth needing to be spoken. On the last night it was incredible. I visited my mom as she sat alone in her room. We embraced. Tomorrow, I'd be on my way. The depth of our faith would carry us through, but this was now; a moment that was like forever.

At Kennedy Airport even though the whole family was there, it was like no one was there but Irene. We embraced and said goodbye. It was like a sledgehammer to my chest. I was in a daze. I was numb. The plane was over Chicago before I felt normal again, realizing that I was on my way to the missions and to a whole new life.

I was heading for the barrios of Mindanao Island in the Philippines. Thirteen thousand miles of cultural difference away. A new language and a new people.

The Philippine Chapter of My Life

The last leg of the long journey was the flight from northern Mindanao to our territory in South Cotabato. We flew over the roughest looking terrain yet. There were dozens of deliberately set forest fires below. Ka-ingan or "slash and burn" fires set by the indigenous people to clear the land of hundreds of years old trees to make room for their little corn fields.

The "first peoples" to come to the islands were still struggling to survive. Every time a new tribe arrived the first settlers got pushed back further into the forest. They never got to learn how to farm for they kept being disenfranchised by the newcomer. Some of the tribes are Magindanaos,

Marinaos, Manobos, Tabolis, Bila'ans, Tasadays and many other forgotten clans.

Banga

The plane was an old DC3. It was familiarly called the yo-yo flight because it was the mail plane and it stopped every fifteen or twenty minutes and landed on a dirt runway. A Philippine Constable arrived at each place with a big gun, bandoliers of bullets and grenades on his belt to receive the mail, then in the shade of the wing he would oversee the sorting of the mail.

At last we were circling over our stop, Lagao (now called General Santos City). Below, the priests of our new Community were eager to greet us as the third batch of missionaries to arrive in Mindanao. It was nice to be welcomed and embraced by a whole new band of brothers.

8,000 islands, 87 languages

One day after I got settled In Lagao, Fr. Jerome Does asked me to do an afternoon mass in a nearby barrio. It was interesting to walk through a very wooded area on the way to the little village. It was the closest thing I ever saw to a jungle.

I heard confessions, offered the Mass and then headed home. But now it was dark. The trail we walked on a few hours earlier seemed very different. It was exciting with strange noises and sights. There was one tree filled with thousands of lightning bugs. It looked like New York City at Christmas time. Our American lightning bugs are loners but here they fly in swarms. It was a very little thing but it was the highlight of my day.

Tagalog language school was my first big challenge. Fr. Ted Walsh and I found ourselves spending many hours every day trying to learn this language that had its roots in Malaysia. After graduating, my first assignment was to a town where nobody spoke that language. They used a Visayan dialect called Ilonggo. I got to work immediately and started memorizing my Sunday sermon in Ilonggo. It was either that or use an interpreter and I did not want to take that route. It was a very good choice because very rapidly I acquired a minimal working knowledge of Ilonggo. Our Bishop, Quentin Olwell, said when he was in China he learned Chinese by simply mastering simple short sermons and doing them over and over again in various places with the help of an informant. I heeded his advice and within six months of hard study I was able to preach my first sermon without reading it. After three years I was able to give my first Passionist Mission in the Ilonggo language. God helped me do this, for back in Brooklyn I failed my Latin Regents exam. I did very poorly in Spanish as well. It must have been the grace of my new vocation for me to learn a new language.

My first permanent parish assignment was in Norala (North Allah). The Pastor was Fr. Justin Garvey who hailed from Oyster Bay, Long Island. He grew up on a big estate. His father was the groundskeeper. Justin was an unusual man. He was a veteran of our mission in China. Every night, when the generator went off, we lit the lantern and got two beers from the kerosene refrigerator. We talked about China and a thousand other things. This was precious sharing time. A great man of God was mentoring me. It was Church history being lived and re-lived each night as we talked.

During my novitiate days in Pittsburgh we prayed every day for Justin to be released from prison. When he finally got out after four years of torture and solitary confinement, I was in awe. He came to visit my class in Jamaica. I think I am a hero worshipper and for sure he was my hero. In the Parish I would unconsciously imitate whatever he would do. The people were in awe, too. He was like an Old Testament patriarch or prophet. However he had a few hang-ups. One was about the men attending the cockfight on Sunday morning. He would blow us all away with his eloquence as he condemned this horrible sin.

Justin Garvey and friend

I enjoyed my time as a parochial vicar. I had no worries or administrative duties to bother about. I concentrated on the language and the people. I visited very many barrios over the next two and a half years. I think these were my happiest days on the missions. Everything was fresh and new and Justin and I got along great.

In our Church we had a very real-looking crucifix with a life-size corpus on it. One day the datu, a local leader of a Bila -an community stopped by to look inside our church. In horror he turned and ran out heading for the market. We ran after him and asked, "What is the matter? Why did you run?" He replied, "There is a dead man hanging up on the wall. He is bleeding." The Bila-an never saw a crucifix before and he was shocked by our life-like depiction of the crucified Jesus. We explained as best we could in that brief encounter.

Fifty wives and a hundred children

An interesting thing about Norala was that it was in the center of the Allah Valley and the Sultan lived in our parish. He was a very busy guy. He had fifty wives to love and one hundred children to feed. His name was Datu Kudanding Kumsah. Education was not too much of a problem. He concentrated only on his number one son. He sent him to our high school. We did the best we could to bring the young man into the twentieth century.

The Fear of God

One memorable barrio call was to a place called Simpsimon. To get there I had to go to the end of town by jeep, then slosh through a swamp and finally hike for a good distance into the village. When I got there, there were only a few little old ladies, some kids, a goat and a few dogs. I think somebody forgot to announce the regular scheduled Mass. I waited for a long time and still nobody came. I was feeling that this was a serious non-response to the Gospel invitation. I had travelled thirteen thousand miles to get here and they did not seem to value what we were bringing to them.

I got the portable Japanese horn and walked through the streets like Jonah. I preached the words of the scripture in a warning to them about the danger of ignoring the good news of Jesus. I proclaimed into the horn as I walked through every street, "**yari na ang ginharian sang Dios, con dili camo magsimba basi ayhan magabut sa inyong barrio ang castigo sang Dios, tungud sa inyong wala nagasimba, maghinulsol kamo!**" Which translated means the equivalent of "repent or else!" Everybody heard it but nothing happened. I returned home after the Mass. I was hot and frustrated with the non-response to my efforts. I felt like "kicking the dust off my shoes."

The next month Justin went to barrio Simpsimon. The whole community was in the chapel this time. The Barrio Captain had a forty-five pistol exposed on his belt. All repented and showed sorrow, it seemed. The barrio captain and many of the elders knew that the missionary has the power to curse the barrio. They know it is real. I did not curse the village but I seriously did warn them not to treat the grace of God carelessly. Justin got home from the barrio very, very late. He was drained. "Owen, what did you say to those people? The whole barrio went to confession! I'm exhausted."

Irene comes for a visit

Justin was not happy when he got the news that the mother of his curate was coming for a visit. His whole image of the foreign missionary was of fifty years ago. This new batch of missionaries was soft. They all had a "Union City mentality." They liked their days off and vacations. The old China hands were tougher and more heroic. And now a mother was coming to visit her son. How embarrassing!

Even though it violated a lot of his myths he turned out to be a wonderful host. A large rice truck was her carriage into the village. She rode up front as the truck splashed through the swollen river. The people cheered and rejoiced at her coming. She said she felt like Jackie Kennedy.

My sister, Bernadette, was her traveling companion. She was quite successful in business and was used to the good life. Some of the people had never seen an American woman before. They were delighted to honor the mother and sister of their foreign priest. That night they put on a program and a fashion show for them. They even gave them lovely gifts.

After the show, Mom and Bernadette went to the nuns' convent to rest. The house was situated right at the end of a huge inundated rice field. Before the show they forgot to pull down the mosquito net and turn off the light. Thousands of bugs from the rice paddies came in, drawn by the light. The white sheets were black with little critters. It was a good while before they could clear the bugs out and go to bed. It was a night to forget.

The next day my sister went on a sick call with me. It was an eye opener for her. The Nipa hut we went into was extremely simple and poor. The sick lady was old and emaciated. The experience was life changing for my sophisticated sibling. She supported my mission heroically ever after.

Garla, A horse in my life.

In the parish we had a fine horse. One day we clocked it going 48 kilometers per hour galloping behind our Land Rover. Our catechist named it GARLA for GARvey and LAlly.

We got word that a lady in Barrio Simpsimon was seriously in trouble; She was bleeding out while delivering her child. I got the Blessed Sacrament, jumped onto Garla and galloped off to the barrio. We seemed to be on eagle's wings. The reality was I was a terrible horseman. When we got into the barrio I could not stop the horse. We passed the house and I shouted out for help. A man bravely reached out and grabbed the reins. I dismounted and went to the dying lady. I gave her the last rites and Holy Communion. She died soon after. It was very sad but I'm glad I got there when I did. She is with the Lord.

POLOMOLOK

I enjoyed Norala and serving with Justin but there is something in the heart of a man that wants his own ship. I was now thirty-three years old and champing at the bit. My father and Bishop Quentin Olwell were classmates at St. Leonard's Academy in Brooklyn. The Bishop was always nice to me. I think I was his fair-haired boy. I was to be the new Pastor of Polomolok.

Barrio leaders at Nocturnal Adoration Procession

In Polomolok I think I was subconsciously still using Justin as my role model. He could get away with cultural mistakes because the people regarded him as a great man. I imitated him but if I made a cultural mistake I'd have to answer for it. I had to grow up fast and do things with greater wisdom.

One Sunday morning, very early, the Judge of the town came to my house. "President Kennedy has been killed". I was shocked. I could not process the horrible news fast enough. Kennedy was also one of my heroes. Six A.M. arrived. It was time now for Mass and the sermon. I knew that JFK was a churchgoer. In the homily I mentioned that and commented that any one who does not go to church is "buang". A word spread through-

Polomolok Parish Center

out town that Fr. Owen implied that the Aglipayans are crazy. They were schismatic Catholics who had no Church building of their own. As a result of my ill chosen word they decided to build a Church. I hated to even look at it after it was built. I paid for not knowing the full meaning of the word "buang"

One day I was driving my truck going south on the National highway (a wide dirt road) to the port city of Dadiangas. I noticed a Jeep coming north with an American in it. I stopped and hailed him down. He introduced himself saying, "Hi, I'm Henry Baldwin from Hawaii and I have come to plant some pineapples here". And plant he did. Rapidly he bought up my entire parish. Dole Philippines began that day.

A Barrio Renewal Mass

The Parish was located at the base of Mount Matutum, a seven thousand foot high inactive volcano. The parish was full of rocks and had no irrigation. The people lived from hand to mouth, as they would say "one scratch, one eat." They were glad to sell their land and get jobs with Dole. Within two years the place was transformed. Earth movers removed the rocks and rearranged the sloping hills and huge artesian wells were drilled. Agro industry in this case turned out to be a win-win situation for everybody.

Upper Klinan was one of last barrios to the south. It was away from the Pineapple growing area and maybe the last acreage to be bought. I was experimenting there with a venture that I called "a barrio renewal week." It was the prototype of the Passionist Barrio mission. It was within the boundaries of my parish and I needed no permissions to try new things. I hired a foreman, and we bought paint, nails and lumber. We found a way of getting the men back to Church. It was right in their culture. It was called bayanihan work. We set a date and provided the Tuba "coconut beer". We had a plan and Mr. Falgui, the foreman, gave the leadership. All work was synchronized with the Mass in the morning and visual aids, confessions and the preaching at night. We had a generator for our power source and fireworks to draw the crowds. It was a bit of new life for a sleepy village and it worked. Almost everybody attended. Something new was being born.

The next barrio was called Polo. It was nearer to the top of the volcano. The same method worked. We were on a roll. One three-day program away from the Poblacion every month, fitted in nicely within the Parish needs. They were all my parishioners and I neglected no one. After seven successful Barrio Renewal Weeks I approached my boss, Fr. Harold Reusch to see if we could start the Passionist Barrio Missions. He loved the idea and said I could polish up my Ilonggo in Iloilo City and after my furlough I could move into the old Saint Gabriel's Seminary building in Lagao and live as a community of two with him. What a great break-through for the Vicariate and the Passionists. But we still had the Bishop to contend with. His priorities were different. He needed to cover the parishes. Thankfully he acceded to our request and gave the venture a six months experimental trial period.

Our General, Theodore Foley, gave us two tasks to perform for the Church. First, establish the diocesan hierarchy (Rome insisted on that) and second establish the Passionist Congregation. We needed two seminaries, a Bishop and eventually a Provincial and Curia. My role in all this was clear to me but not to too many others. A mission band of itinerant preachers would attract vocations to the Passionists and would be a specific apostolic mode of priesthood very distinct from the diocesan parish clergy. It would help us to establish the Congregation of the Passion. I was extraordinarily motivated to do this work.

When I returned from my furlough in September, I went immediately to St. Gabriel's, our first mission community house. It was the Feast of the Exaltation of the Holy Cross and Harold asked me to be the principal celebrant. In those days we were not accustomed to preach at every Mass. Harold was surprised. I preached with great unction to my one-man congregation on this our very special Feast of the Exaltation of the Cross. It meant a great deal to me and Harold was surprised to hear what I saw happening with us. To him it had simply been his residence and now he'd be sharing it with me. In reality, I believe it was our first Intentional Local Passionist Community in this part of the world.

Our first barrio mission was in Busok, a place far off the beaten path. It was across the Banga River and a good hike into the village. Fr. Harold Reusch was very late getting to our agreed on meeting place. We left word that we had to go ahead because the whole village would be waiting us. We would send a guide back for him.

He insisted on coming with us because he said this new experiment should have a superior at the helm. It was a new outreach. Well, the opening of the mission was exciting. We were all caught up in the moment. Our first night was a success. It was 9:00 P.M. before we thought of Harold who was now fuming in Frank's parish house several miles away. The convento boy headed out to get the boss. They got back after 10:00 P.M. Harry was very upset. He asked me to follow him into a grass hut loaned to us for the duration of the mission. He scolded me for starting the mission without a superior. He gave me a penance like we used to get in the novitiate. He told me to place my fingers beneath my knees and say the Our Father and Hail Mary and Gloria five times. The bamboo floor was quite hard and I felt the physical pain in my hands but I felt the humiliation more.

Outdoor Stations of the Cross; Harold and I

After the penance was over we sat down to plan for the next day. By the grace of God we let go of the whole mishap. We simply had a bad start. Later on I could laugh at the entire affair whenever I told the story. The elements of the exercises of the mission were all very blessed and I felt anointed for this new work. I was overjoyed.

This is the way we did the missions. One week before the mission team arrived in the place our advance man went ahead to prepare the people for the event. He visited every house in the village.

In Busok, he got all the children to meet us at the river and hike to the chapel with the team while skyrockets would signal to the barrio folks that we were coming. St. Paul of the Cross used to ring a hand bell.

When we would get to the chapel, the mission began with the first talk being focused on the children's needs. We also asked the children from the far away places in the mountains to tell their parents to come to the barrio chapel for the catechetical slide show, confessions and the mission sermon. It worked well. Ninety-eight percent of the barrio people attended the mission. The skyrockets and the generator-powered sound system worked wonderfully to attract the crowds. Besides, we were the only show in town. The people in the faraway villages seldom got to church in the Poblacion. So the mission was geared to make up for what was lacking in their lives.

On Thursday night we focused on the Last Supper and the Mass, with twelve leaders of the Barrio dressed like the apostles. On Friday morning, the Purpose of Life. In the evening the Passion with Living Stations and the men carrying a large heavy cross around the barrio, with their sins nailed to the wood. Saturday morning, the Resurrection and at night Mary's Role in our Salvation and a Rosary Procession.

Jesus enters Jerusalem

On Sunday, Pentecost with the final Mass being offered for their deceased loved ones. Wow!

After the mission Harold and I celebrate

What God did in those four days was terrific! Harry and I sang "the Sound of Music" all the way to Marbel. The hills were alive. I really felt like the Barrio mission was the most effective ministry imaginable. I was willing to do this for the rest of my life.

"I have come to light a fire on the earth. How I wish the blaze were ignited." (Luke 12:49).

I desire to make these words of Jesus, my own.

An evening mission in Barrio Bula

But God had other plans for me. I was only able to do eleven more barrio missions before Fr. Tom

Carroll got hepatitis. The Bishop told Fr. Harold that that was the end of the attempt at a mission band for the barrios.

I had eagerly desired to become pastor of my first parish assignment of Polomolok but now I was mourning my assignment to this next parish. The novelty of being Pastor had worn off. I remember the ride north on the bus. My heart was very heavy.

I was assigned to be the pastor of Banga, a municipality of about 400 square miles, 21 barrios of about 1,500 people each and a population center of 11,000 people called the Poblacion. A total of about 51,000 Catholics, several thousand Christians of other traditions and an unknown number of Muslims and aborigines.

Imagine trying to take care of 51,000 parishioners!

One day, Fr. Eugene Leso of Kiamba needed help in Maasin,one of his coastal barrios. I said OK. Together we did 32 weddings and 80 baptisms at their fiesta. On another day, I helped the bishop as he confirmed 1,300 of our children. The numbers were incredible. Mass, of course, was the most precious element of the ministry. Two a day and three on Sundays and we preached every chance we could get. Sometimes we had three unscheduled funerals a day and we preached at every one of them because some in the congregation might never be in Church again until they would be carried in for their own funeral.

First People

Pastoral methods were quite important in mission parish work. Thank God for what I learned at New York Life about methodology. Banga was as big as some dioceses in Ireland. I really needed help. There were no priests available. I even went to Ireland looking for priests with Bishop Quentin's permission. I visited twenty-two counties and got not a single priest. However the solution was right in front of my nose.

In every parish there were devout Catholic teachers who work in the Public Schools. They were allowed to take one-year leave of absence without pay. All I needed to do was pay their salary. With help from home I could swing it.

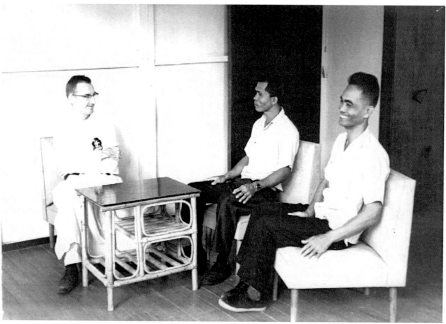

Agriculturist and Parish Manager

I found a beautifully gifted man who wished to help. Rody Dorado was married and had three fine kids. He became my partner in mission. We did great things together. He could preach, teach and manage far better than I could. What a gift! He became like a brother to me.

The year flew by and Rody had to go back to his teaching job but a pattern was set. Each year, find another good man who was a potential partner in mission for me. One year we had Mr. Solivio and then the following year we got Mr. Santa Maria. It was good for them all and great for me. It was another win-win situation.

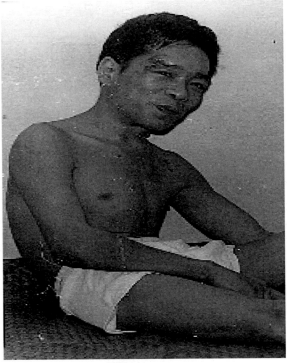

Vicente

One day Vicente was at my back door. He was a quadriplegic. Only his left arm worked. He used it to drag his whole body along. He lived in the dumps and ate whatever he could scrounge. His body was full of worms and he had TB. He had come to the Church to attend the mission being given by the Redemptorists. When I saw him I knew that I had to do something. Most surely I would meet him on judgment day one way or another. I took him in and with the help of the entire parish staff we made him feel at home. We built him a little house with a tile floor and water seal toilet. Later on we put together a wheelchair much in the style of the Flintstones. We instructed him in the faith and helped him get ready for his first Holy Communion. People donated some nice clothes and he became beloved by many of the parishioners. Word spread even to the mountain people and even they talked about Vicente.

The chief of the Bila-an village came down the mountain to see me. He was holding an infant whose mother had died in childbirth. The malnourished child was covered with sores on her body and scales on her scalp. It was a pitiful sight. The chief thought that we took in abandoned people and so we now had an infant. If we did not take it in, it would have been abandoned. Luckily one of the parishioners was looking to adopt a baby. We helped the couple to take over. A year or two later the couple brought the baby back for a visit. She was a little chubby, had on a pretty pink dress, white shoes, she had a ribbon in her shiny hair. She was lovely. I thought that this is what happens to us when God adopts us into His family.

One day my legs gave out. I was bone tired. I experienced what Bishop Walsh of Maryknoll once said, "The dark night of the soul for the Missionary is exhaustion.

Furlough

In 1965 I went home on furlough. I rested continuously for six weeks on the living room couch. After a while some energy came back and I decided I needed to do something. I signed up at a gym and tried to build up my body for my next lap in the missions.

I also made a Cursillo, a little course in Christianity, which had its origins in Spain. It was being given down on Court St. in Brooklyn by a very anointed team of priests and lay people. It would change my life. Thank you, Lord!

One of the big elements of the program was the Palanca. It was a penance that someone would perform for you so that you would make a good retreat. I had no one to sponsor me, so a Puerto Rican gentleman volunteered to help me. In the middle of the program there was time set aside for the reading of the 'love letters' containing the palanca sacrifices offered up by the sponsors. My letter read, "For the priest who has no sponsor I will offer up three nights of sleeping on chickpeas in my bed and for three days I will walk with gravel in my shoes." I was very touched by his sacrifice. Later on at the closing I would share what it meant to me.

At my cursillo worktable the participants were very ordinary men. One was a sanitation worker, one was a mathematician, another was a laborer, and one a white-collar worker. Each table group took turns and prayed audibly before the Blessed Sacrament. Something happened to me as I said my prayer. I think I was being consciously immersed into Jesus for the first time. It felt like I was being born again. And it has stayed with me over forty years. Again I say, thank You, Lord!

At the Cursillo graduation ceremony on Sunday afternoon many former graduates were in attendance. Each new cursillista was invited to share a high point of his retreat. When it got to me I was overwhelmed. I said, "My greatest moment was when the letter was read saying that a complete stranger walked on gravel and slept on chick peas for me. St. Paul of the Cross would be moved to tears when he thought of what Jesus did for him. "Imagine, God died for me," he cried! I never wept over the nails driven into Jesus' hands and the spikes piercing His feet for me. But I did weep when the letter was read saying that the Puerto Rican man walked on stones for me and slept on chickpeas for me. The tears were like a second baptism for me. I have wept over Jesus' love for me many times since.

As a pastoral method I believed that the Cursillo was a must for Banga and the whole of the South Cotabato. Therefore when Bishop Olwell announced that we would start the Cursillo in our prelature I was happy to collaborate. Thank you

Lord for his initiative, for that meant I did not have to lead it. If he did not start it though, I would have had to do it in Banga. At the time, it was the perfect instrument. Nothing is more powerful than an idea whose time has come. It was time to re-evangelize a baptized society that was never adequately instructed in the faith. The people were cultural Catholics and they believed in Jesus. That was not a bad place to start.

There were a good number of English-speaking professional people to start with. Fr. Zacharias Statkun, under the bishop, assumed the leadership of this new movement. We had very different personality types and we approached the little course in Christianity in completely different ways. The format and details were very important to Zach. To me, not so. Unfortunately we did not agree on many things.

After about a year or so he ran out of English speakers. The Cursillo movement seemed to be finished. What to do? I had thousands of farmers who spoke only Ilonggo and who wanted to take the little course in Christianity but there was no Ilonggo speaking team to conduct it.

Then I heard that the cursilistas of Iloilo City up in Panay had solved the problem. They translated all the talks into the vernacular and adapted many other elements to accommodate to the culture.

I got news that the team from Iloilo was coming down to M'lang in Northern Cotabato to conduct the Cursillo, which now had a new name. It was called the Sa-Maria Movement. It was a great idea but the English-speaking group of cursilistas in Marbel would not recognize this new version because it did not follow the Cursillo system to the letter.

In my opinion, good missiology demanded that we adapt for the non-English speakers. At first we did not see the ramifications in all of this so we just blissfully went ahead and turned out about two hundred spiritually renewed Sa-Marians every month. The candidates came from all over the vicariate. It was the hottest thing in Mindanao. We had overflow crowds at each opening night. Eventually we began the program for women.

One lady came and demanded to be let in to the program even though there was no more room in the inn. She threatened to kill somebody if we did not let her in. She said she really needed to make a retreat. She went across the plaza to get drunk so that she would have the courage to kill one of us if we refused her. We had no police that we could call on so we decided to let the gal in. Amazingly she did not hurt anyone. She made a good retreat. She was healed, forgiven and was spiritually awakened and retuned home, praising God. She really took the kingdom of heaven by storm. God is kind and merciful!

The Rural Development Movement

Wonder Corn

The New People's Army was a Communist group that was perpetually causing unrest in the north. The discontent was even beginning to upset some our people in the south.

Pope Paul VI sent Msgr. Liguti of the American Grange to foster the Rural Development Movement in our place. A convention was organized with every Diocese and Vicariate participating.

I was very interested in learning ways of improving the economics of our folks for that was the bottom line of our problem and the Communists were harping on that. Long story short, this new emphasis distracted me. Within a year I had 15 different social action projects going on in the parish. An agriculturist, a social worker, a doctor, and a credit union manager were now on the payroll. Our parish classes were on Miracle Rice, Wonder Corn, home vegetable gardens, livestock upgrades and irrigation projects. It was all very exciting for a city boy like me. I was really caught up with it all.

Bishop Quentin C.P.

One day the bishop sent a letter to us stating that the International Pilgrim Virgin Statue was coming to our area. If we wanted to have the statue make a visit to our mission, we should simply sign up and it would happen for us. I read the letter and put it aside. I really did not have time for a visit by a visiting priest with a statue of the Blessed Mother. The letter got misplaced.

The Pilgrim Virgin

The arrival day came. I remembered that the Bishop wanted me to send a delegation to meet the statue at the airport. I quickly got a jeep full of parish workers and we arrived at the airport just in time. More than 1,000 people were there. They were praying and singing with great devotion. My group and I were there because we did not want to get in trouble with the bishop.

The plane landed. The door opened. The Board Member of the Province was there. He came carrying the Pilgrim Virgin statue in his own arms. The people began singing, "Ave, Ave, Ave Maria!" The Holy Spirit was convicting me. A gift of tears flooded my soul. The people back in my parish would have loved this grace but I failed to announce the event. The more beautiful the singing got, the worse I felt.

The motorcade to Marbel was getting ready to depart. My town was really nearby, just a half mile off the main highway. I asked Fr. Cyprian Regan to please drive through my town but he said, "no! you had your chance." I really blew it for everybody. I was very sorry.

Fr. Patrick Moore of he Scarbhoro Fathers of Canada saw my face and I think he understood what I was going through. Quietly and before we started moving, Fr. Moore in the lead vehicle asked Fr. Cyprian to please honor my request. Cyprian reluctantly agreed. In the meantime, I had climbed up onto the back of the lead truck where the statue was enthroned. The huge motorcade began to head eastward on the dusty road. When we came to the turnoff into my town I was amazed.

The lead truck and the entire motorcade made the turn. In a few moments we were circling the Banga plaza amid a huge cloud of dust. The spectators in the town were mystified to see me and this strange sight filling the town. We did not stop. It was just an unscheduled "fly by" to bless the town. It really touched my soul and I wept as we continued on over the mountain to Marbel. When we reached the main road, I saw that there was an arch that the people had built. They lined up on both sides of the road. Their great devotion to Our Lady made me feel embarrassed and ashamed.

I decided to stay in the Cathedral and pray with all the people from Marbel. I stayed until after dark. Finally Fr. Moore came on the scene.

He said, "Aren't you the priest who got zapped at the airport?" I said, "Yes" and told him what had happened. He asked if I wanted the Pilgrim Virgin to visit my Parish in the morning and again I said "Yes." It was Saturday night and he would be leaving for the airport early in the morning, He said he would come by my church at about 6:30 A.M. Our main Mass was at 6 A.M. "Preach till I get there," he said. "Tell the people what happened. I will preach when I get there." And preach he did! He prophesied that a miracle of grace would happen in our parish.

In the next two years, through the SA Maria movement, we had about 3,000 people come back to the sacraments. It was like our own "Guadalupe experience." One Sunday, there were so many communions that I almost fainted in the heat from fatigue. I had to ask one of the nuns to continue to distribute Holy Communion for me. (This was before we had Eucharistic ministers.)

New Spans on the Church

The SA-Maria Retreats continued marvelously well and I think things got a little more balanced after Our Lady's visit. Before her arrival, I had become like a Peace Corps Worker instead of an apostolic missionary.

But subplots to my story were beginning to emerge.

One of the local doctors was beginning to see a drop off in the number of his patients. Our clinic was causing him to lose money. He was not happy. To confront me one day he got drunk and came over to my compound with gun drawn. He screamed at the nuns, "Where is that alien priest?" Luckily, I was not home but he made it clear to the Sisters that this was not the last we would hear from him.

A short time later I got a scary unsigned letter in cutout form saying, "For 100 pesos your clinic will burn and for 500 pesos YOU WILL DIE!" And then the stones banging on my roof at night began to terrify me. I started taking sleeping pills so I could sleep but nothing seemed to help. The joy from my other success stories began to fade. What good would it all matter if I was dead?

Another subplot to my story was because an overflow of our SA Maria Movement spread to the other parishes.

People started coming from all over to attend our program and returned to their own parishes spiritually on fire, saying to their own pastors, "Here I am...how can I help you?" My priest confreres did not know how to deal with this modal change in their parishioners and did not feel comfortable with the whole situation since they were not in on the planning.

After two years the problem of division in the prelature reached major proportions. Unity is essential in the Church and in no way did I intend to bring division. However, a split was truly a serious reality now. How did it happen and how could we stop it? Most said, merge the two movements. Others said, foster the one and let the other fade away. There were no more English-speaking candidates for the Cursillo anyway. I loved the cultural and linguistic adaptation that the SA Maria programs had adopted. It was perfect missiology as far as I could see. The English-speaking professional community did not agree with me. Some said I was the problem since I sided with the Ilonggos. To make a long story short, I felt I could not bring about unity the way the administrators wanted it. It was not a matter of disobedience. **I was not the man for the job.**

They agreed I had to go. I was to be transferred to Manila. Fr. Edward Deviny would take over Banga and the Father Tony Magbanua, an Ilonggo secular priest, would lead the SA Maria Movement.

I had an unusual relationship with the people of Banga and this transfer would not be easy for me or for them. I had grown to love the folks very much and I knew they loved me. One day the mayor and judge of the town even invited me to become a Filipino citizen. I was honored and pondered the offer for a long time.

My Brother Priests

A year previously, on Holy Thursday, as all the priests gathered for the blessing of the oils with Bishop Olwell, he said that he was, as bishop, married to the territory and its entire people. It was the nature of things. I was really moved by the thought of this relationship. After a lot of prayer I decided to marry my parish. Banga would be my bride. In my heart during a deep prayer time one day I told the Lord that I consented to this new way of relating. After that all kinds of good things began to happen. I felt that God had blessed me for my offering. Even my preaching improved. I was loving my spouse every time I preached or did anything for anyone. The people felt my love. They would do anything for me.

Fr. Harold asked me not to tell anyone about my transfer. I tried to be quiet about it but my secretary got wind of the move and he told a lot of people. They had a meeting among themselves and they decided to send a delegation to the acting Bishop, Fr. Justin Garvey. (Bishop Olwell had just retired). They wanted to ask him to keep me in Banga. They used a method that was popular in the Cursillo Movement. They would rise early and all go the Bishop's residence to sing the Mananita, a tender lullaby used to show love and respect.

It was about 4 A.M. A whole bunch of rice trucks pulled up at the Bishop's residence. They lit candles and began to serenade Fr. Justin. Strangely enough this was a frightening experience for Fr. Justin for he knew nothing of this custom.

He had been a missioner in China and he was a little bit apprehensive about a lot of things. It might have been a touch of post-traumatic stress disorder. He had been arrested and brutally tortured. He was in solitary confinement for a long time. For him, this middle of the night visit, was a nightmare and I think he must have panicked. He came out of his house and found Mayor Improgo and Judge Naraval and many people with lighted "torches". He scolded them all and presumed that I put them up to this drama. He was quite upset to say the least. I knew nothing of this whole thing. I was home twelve miles over the mountain, totally unaware of what was happening. I was sound asleep.

At sunrise back in Banga I heard a motorcade of rice trucks filled with parishioners. They pulled up outside my window. I got up and went out and found a lot of people weeping. They told me what had happened. I figured out what would happen next. I would be transferred that very day.

We prepared for my 'last supper.' We all went into the Church. I vested for Mass and the singing began as I recited the prayers. By now I too was deeply moved. I would never see these wonderful people again. It was like a divorce being forced upon me because of my vow of obedience.

As I guessed it, a telegram arrived from Fr. Harold, the religious superior, saying, "It's over! Leave the mission when my Jeep gets there. Don't even pack". Obviously a great misunderstanding was in progress. From Fr. Justin's interpretation of the events I was at fault. Fr. Harold did not see what had happened. It was high drama. A comedy of errors but it wasn't funny. I was really very hurt. The next morning I was on my way to Manila. Philippine Airlines was on strike. I found myself looking out from the stern of a cargo ship as it set sail from the port of Dadiangas. My beloved Mindanao was fading away from my sight. I had given it eight years of my life. I understood the culture somewhat and I had tried to learn the language. I did my best.

Luzon

As I sailed for a couple of days, I was getting my thoughts together. What had just happened? Was it anybody's fault? I don't think so! I think it was a Divine set up to get me into the next chapter of my story.

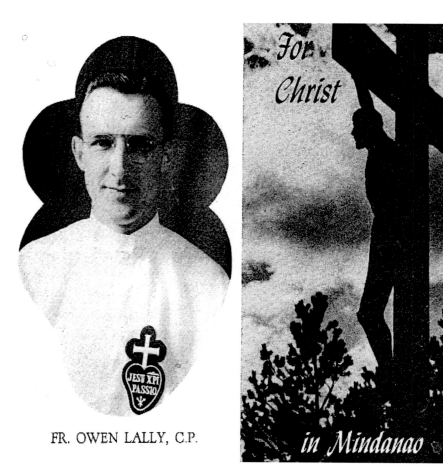

FR. OWEN LALLY, C.P.

For Christ

in Mindanao

"For who has known the mind of God or who has been his counsellor? How inscrutable are His judgements and how unsearchable are His ways". (Romans 11: 35)

What shall I do? I could give missions in Panay, Romblon and Negros Island where the Ilonggos came from. That seemed to give me hope and my depression began to lift. I could get back to the mission band but on a bigger scale. The Visayan Islands could be my field of mission endeavor.

When God closes one door, He opens another. I felt a bit excited over this new possibility. I needn't look back to find my joy. God has a plan for me. All I need do is find it. "I know the plans I have for you," says the Lord, "not for your woe but for your well-being."

A couple of days later we were pulling into the harbor of Manila Bay. A fairly modern city opened up for me. English was the language I would speak here. I did not work in the Tagalog dialect that I had studied at first. In many ways it was a relief to just think and speak in English.

I moved into our theology house and tried to get adjusted to a new way of life. The roads were paved and the amenities of a big city were open to me. I spent a few days exploring my new environment. It was very interesting. Mindanao had not been on the tourist trail but Manila was. I liked it.

Mother Madeline, provincial superior of the Sisters of St. Paul de Chartres, had a need. She had a whole bunch of Sisters' retreats lined up all over the country. The preacher got seriously sick. Could I help?

God was wasting no time in putting me back to work. But I had no experience or sermons to draw on. Sister said I had 30 days to get ready. Three major talks a day plus a daily homily for 10 days. Wow! I was going to have to dig deep. I had been overactive in the parish for a long time but now I had to think and write about the contemplative religious life. There were ten retreats to be given and an average of fifty sisters on each one.

There was a beautiful quiet cemetery about a mile from my house. I went there each morning and prayed and focused for a couple of hours on one subject Then I went home, had something to eat, took a quick siesta and then I began to write down my thoughts on a yellow pad. Considering all the talks, I had to produce one talk a day for 30 days. With the homilies I would have to do the best I could with them when the time came. I'd had plenty of practice with that from my time in South Cotabato. I had given a homily almost twice a day for the past eight years.

Mother Madeline

The first retreat was up north in the city of Tugagerao. These nuns were all college teachers and they were very smart. My first talk put them to sleep. One young sister approached me later and begged me to change my style. I had chosen to imitate what the Passionist preachers used to do in our retreat houses back home. They would sit at a table with a little lamp and read their material.

I discovered a lecture hall, which was like an amphitheater. I used the blackboard. I wrote out my entire talk in outline form. And when I spoke I tried to be very animated. I used a lot of body language. The sisters were able to stay awake.

In addition to the talks I had to be available to see each sister for a private conference and confession during the retreat. At the end of the retreat Mother Madeline invited me to do the next retreat on her list. I was very happy but I was exhausted.

When I got back to the theology house in Manila, I realized my body was full of pain. I ached all over. This Sister's retreat was tougher than anything I ever attempted in Mindanao. I think that the mental pain was the greatest. I was prayed out and talked out. Sleep would not take away the feeling.

I decided to go to swimming and later go to a few movies. After a couple of days of R&R I seemed to be coming back to life. It was like a mini furlough. The only trouble was that none of the other priests could take time off from their work to be with me. This is the lot of the itinerant missionary. By its nature it is a manic depressive sort of life. "Lord, hold me close! Don't let go of me, please!"

Between retreats I tried to get back down to the Visayan Islands to do a couple of missions in the Ilonggo dialect. I did not want to lose the language from lack of use. I did some missions on Panay, one in Mambusao and one each in Sigma and Jamindan. Eventually the other works got in the way. The bigger mission band had opportunities galore. I could not resist some of the requests that were coming in now. It was a mission band of one.

A Vacation

Oh happy day! I found a companion to travel with me, Fr. Cyprian Regan. We flew to Batangas to visit the cone shaped Mayon Volcano and the hot bubbling springs. Sulfur fumes rose up all around us and we could not stay very long. We enjoyed looking at the volcano but we had to move on. We got the plane to the Mountain Province but it caught fire and we had to return to Batangas.

We changed planes and eventually got to Baguio. It is the only real cool area in the Philippines. The American Army used it after the war for R & R for the soldiers after things settled down a bit. It was nicely developed. After that we boarded a Dangwa Tranco bus and headed up to a road that took us up to about seven or eight thousand feet to the Bontok area to see the Igorot people. They are a tribe that used to be headhunters and cannibals. They still wear their native dress in most places; loincloths for the men and the ladies wear an interestingly patterned abaca skirt. One place I remember was the traditional storytelling fireplace. Bare footprints were worn into the smooth rock platforms. The native men had been squatting nightly on the same spot for over 5,000 years.

All was great except for the bug I caught along the way. I ended up in the Bontoc Hospital for a day or two. All in all the vacation was fascinating. I was so glad Cyprian said yes to the adventure.

The Asian Social Institute

During one of my retreats to the communities of Sisters of St. Paul I met a nun whose blood sister worked as the assistant to the Director of the graduate school of the Asian Social Institute. I was offered an office space free of charge for my research into pastoral methods. It was an opportunity for me to get a place of focus for the social and pastoral aspects of my work. I am not sure that the Spirit led this venture because at that juncture I did not know the Spirit very well. It just looked like a good opportunity for whatever and the price was right. From here I could do some research. I was my own boss.

I asked Fr. Harold, for a spiritual sabbatical and he consented. It would just be for an extra ninety days tacked on to my three-month regular furlough, which was coming soon. I began with a

40-day house of prayer experience at our Passionist House of Greater Solitude in Birmingham, Alabama. It was a great experience. I had been almost 10 years being overactive. The contemplative side of my vocation had been neglected. At the end of my forty days I needed more prayer. I found a place where they actually train people to run houses of prayer. This was the pastoral method that really appealed to me. It was the Kresge House of Prayer in Detroit. I made a reservation for the following month.

The Western Hemisphere

I had a trip planned to study the best foreign missions in South America. The Latin American Bureau in Washington planned it for me.

My sisters, Bernadette, Claire and Anita ran a little card party to help with my expenses. They raised exactly the amount that was needed for my airplane ticket. It was like a little sign of affirmation that I was possibly on the right track.

I started out making a pilgrimage to Guadalupe all by myself. It was a large-scale reminder of what happened in Banga with the three thousand people who came back to the sacraments. I was grateful.

There was a place for anthropology studies in Mexico City. The Government ran it. There are many tribes in the Andes, all of which had there own "old testaments" made up of legends, myths and possibly some true natural revelation. Our Christian New Testament is the fulfillment of all their "old testaments". They had their gods and demons. They needed to have the revelation of Jesus. For me it was a great metaphor for the process that was going on all over the world in the religions of the world.

My next stop was Ocosinco, in Chiapas. It was a Franciscan mission. They were doing some excellent work training leaders for the barrios. And then I went on to Bachahon run by the Jesuits. They actually trained local married leaders up to the point of ordination, as only they can.

My next stop was Guatemala. I arrived at the Maryknoll mission in Huehuetenango. All of a sudden everything stopped and everybody moved into deception mode. The army trucks were coming to "conscript" their young men into the army. When they arrived there was not one young man to be found. All had a preplanned hiding place and it was great to see the community at work to protect its young.

Panama, Colombia, Ecuador, Peru, Chile, Argentina, Uruguay, Brazil all had something interesting going on. Most of it boiled down to the ministries of the basic Christian communities, a pastoral method which the whole world must eventually discover. I saw great attempts to be an authentic local manifestation of the Risen Body of Christ. They had the structure and the theory but I did not see any major acts of the Holy Spirit yet. Next stop, America del Norte.

Detroit

I was feeling vulnerable and weak after my trip. I also had accumulated a huge amount of weariness from my first 10 years on the missions. I felt positive about my vocation but I had fears about the future. The work was really beyond me. The loneliness was an awesome challenge and I was frightened. I told the sisters at the house of prayer that I needed a complete overhaul. I needed to charge my batteries, renew my cylinders and change my oil. They looked at me with fear not knowing how to help me.

Then came a Sister in with some good news. Her name was Sister Elizabeth. She was on the Council of her Order and she was doing some research on houses of prayer. She would be leaving the next day. She was just passing through. She was not on the staff. I told her of my needs and she lit up. She told me all about the Catholic Pentecostal Movement and she thought it would help me. I was glad to find out that there was something that could help me but I was terrified of what people would say.

In my town of Banga we had some Pentecostals. They were a bit much. Also my religious community might laugh me to scorn. Some of the men called them "jump up" churches. Could I handle the criticism that was bound to come? At this juncture it was either the charismatic movement or my mission vocation. It was a deep grace I was being offered and I knew I should not refuse it. God was calling me to it.

Sister Elizabeth told me and all the other retreatants that she was going to make a prayer vigil in the Chapel. She would be there at 2 A.M. If anyone wanted to pray to be baptized in the Spirit and in fire they could come and pray for it with her. We then retired to our rooms. I knew that this would be the last night I would be a normal Catholic priest. I set my clock and went to bed filled with apprehension and anticipation.

I got to the chapel at 2 A.M. (a good "Passionist hour" for at that time it was our customary time of prayer). The others were there praying quietly. After a while, Sister Elizabeth invited us to pray with her one by one. Then she laid hands on my head and prayed in tongues. I agreed with her prayer for a release of the Holy Spirit within me. The experience was quiet and lasted only a few moments. I felt nothing but peace and I wondered if anything happened inside me. Then she moved on to the others. Some of them prayed in tongues and some prophesied. Others were deeply touched. I wanted a sign of some sort. Who would believe me unless some manifestation of the Spirit was present in me? I knew this grace was not just for me. After a while we went back to our rooms to complete our night sleep.

I woke up early. The first thought I had was that all foreign missioners in the world should come home and receive the Spirit, as Jesus said, "Wait in the city and THEN you will be my witnesses to the ends of the earth."

When I went down for breakfast I learned that Sister Elizabeth had already left. I never saw her again. "No one knows where the Spirit comes from or where it goes."

It troubled me a bit that the gift of praying in tongues was not given to me. I mentioned this to one of the sisters who did receive it and she said to read and pray Matthew 7 and Luke 11 until I get it. "Ask and you shall receive. Seek and you shall find. Knock and it shall be opened unto you." For the next few weeks I did this whenever I could.

One day an invitation came to concelebrate with the members of an ecumenical house of prayer. A Marist brother was the vicar, an Anglican was in charge of the kitchen, a Lutheran priest (validly ordained in Scandinavia) was the coordinator and an Assembly of God minister was a spiritual counselor, two others were participants. There were six in all. Cardinal Deardon had given his blessing to this project and permission to concelebrate to any visiting priest. Seeking unity in a Christian community fascinated me.

The Mass began. The readings were shared. The homily was anointed, as was everything else. The Consecration was very real and finally the kiss of peace came. The anointing was so strong that I think I was in an altered state of consciousness. The communion was beautiful. And the ceremony came to an end too soon.

We all went to the living room of the house. Hors d'oeuvres were served. Glasses of wine presented. When they got to me I took the wine. I put it to my lips but put it back on the tray. I did not want it. I was drunk already from the Mass. I have never taken a drink since. It was in 1971.

I think it was a special gift to me for my vocation. The Irish Virus was in my family and I'm sure I am predisposed to the disease. Total abstinence was an unasked for gift. I'll take it Lord. Thank You for all the trouble you've saved me.

Back to the Missions

Finally, my furlough came to an end and I was on my way back to the Philippines. I was in the town of Namur in Belgium. I was making a little pilgrimage to the birthplace of St. Julie Billiart, the foundress of the Sisters of Notre Dame de Namur. Sister Rosemary Davis SNDN of the staff at Kresge House was going to come later to help with the Charismatic work in the missions.

I was staying in a little hotel in town. I was alone. I was saying Mass in my room and after communion I was saying to the Lord that if there was anything in my heart that I had not repented of, I do so now. All of a sudden the gift of tongues came over me. I felt the anointing. I yielded to it for a good while. It seemed like something very normal was happening to me. It was the zenith or apex of my entire spiritual life. Thank you, Jesus!

The next day I went to Amsterdam to get my plane to Bangkok and the Philippines. It was a partial charter flight for returning missionaries.

The night before the flight I remember walking around the block near the hotel. It was raining. I tried to pray in the new prayer language. To my surprise and delight it kicked in again. I discovered that I could pray this way any time I wanted to even if I was dry and distracted.

Next evening I was on a K.L.M. 747 flying over the desert towards India. The Holy Spirit came over me without me praying for it. The prayer gift came on strong. I was embarrassed, so I got up and went into the bathroom to pray. I prayed for India. I prayed for Asia and the Philippines till we got to Thailand. After a night of rest in Bangkok I got another plane to Hong Kong.

On the plane, I sat next to an Irish nun from Kilkenny. I shared my story. The Holy Spirit started to come down on her. She began to get flushed and somewhat embarrassed. What was happening to her? I believe that her life would never be the same. "Praise God from whom all blessings flow."

New Life

The Philippine Catholic Church was, it seemed, a sleeping giant and was not too effectual at that time. I thought that the kingdom of darkness had nothing to fear. But to wake a sleeping giant was another thing altogether. That I think is where I came into the picture.

There was only one other Catholic priest in the Islands familiar with the Charismatic Movement and he was down in Leyte and was doing little to promote this movement of the Holy Spirit. There were two Mary knoll Sisters in Quezon City who prayed with a Pentecostal couple but they saw nothing great on the horizon for the Catholic Church. I think I was the only one who saw it as a huge happening about to unfold.

I threw myself into this new Movement and was out every night visiting some convent or seminary proclaiming the good news of the New Pentecost. One day I was riding in the back of a crowded Jeepny (A rebuilt surplus jeep). It came to me what an awesome task was ahead of me. I was the only priest in Manila that I knew of, with this gift alive and surging within his breast.

Mrs. Yusay

I was visiting the sick one day at Makati Medical Center. A young girl approached and asked if I would anoint her auntie who was dying. The lady had cancer of the liver. When I got there she was spitting up bile and things looked very bad for her. I asked Sister Rosemary to join me. We prayed over Mrs. Yusay and we immediately felt the Holy Spirit at work in us. Heat, "pins and needles" surged within our hands and then all became very quiet. Mrs. Yusay was miraculously healed. She was released and went home after just three days of observation. She witnessed to all she met how Jesus healed her. The word spread fast and people praised God for His wonderful works.

For years in the parish I anointed people. God did his powerful thing always but this was different. The charismatic gift of healing and miracles was at work, doing "signs and wonders" to show that His kingdom was coming. The reign of God was at hand.

I notified Cardinal Santos. He said, through his secretary, that I did not need permission to pray with people. I just wanted him to know that this was something big and he should know about it.

Then all heaven broke loose. Within a month, people were inviting the Holy Spirit into their lives from all walks of life, rich and poor alike.

One day, a chauffeured black car pulled into my backyard. The Papal Nuncio came to meet this "priest that was stirring things up all over the city". I was not home at the time but Fr. Ronan Callahan was. I think He almost had a heart attack over this encounter with the Pope's representative. I'm sorry I missed the excitement.

A New Pentecost... Without a doubt!

Extraordinary things started to happen. One day at the S.V.D. seminary in the town of Tagaytay, fifty miles to the south, I was explaining to the novices about the renewal of the Sacrament of Confirmation. I told them when I was about twelve years old the sisters at my grammar school told me about what to expect in the Sacrament of Confirmation. Peace, love, joy and the other fruits of the spirit, but they failed to tell me about the power gifts of prophecy, healing, miracles and the gift of praying in tongues. I also knew my aunt was coming to visit and I expected that she would give me five dollars. I got what I expected but not all that the Sacrament potentially had for me.

Then I told the novices what happened in Detroit. I asked them to meet me in the chapel after supper if they wanted with expectant faith, to renew their confirmation. Everybody showed up, even Fr. Adolf Milder S.V.D. the German master of novices. I simply read Acts 2:2-4, preached briefly and laid hands on each novice. What followed was incredible. It was like the first Pentecost. Tongues, prophecy, visions, sung litanies and ecstasies occurred. Then it went into worship, which lasted for three hours. Finally Fr. Mildner said to me, "Fr. Owen, how do you stop this? I said, "I don't know." But after a while things quieted down.

I was staying down the road so I went back to the convent where I was giving a retreat. The Franciscan Missionaries of Mary had invited me to give the final week of their four-week renewal program for their foreign missionaries from all over Southeast Asia. Fr. Cassian Yuhas C.P. had given the first week. They were really ready for the coming of the Spirit and so was I ready for more.

At my opening conference a few days before, I opened my mouth and nothing came out. I could not talk. Nothing was coming forth. It felt like the "well was dry." I asked them to pray over me. The Spirit started moving again. The extraordinary happening that followed, I believe was from God. I am convinced it was not from me. Eventually, after a short talk, the Spirit gave the sisters the gift of singing in tongues. It was beautiful and heavenly.

That night I retired very early because I suspected that the Seminary priests down the road would be coming back. Sure enough, I had been sleeping a short while when I heard their Volkswagen Combie outside my cottage. It was about 9 P.M. It was Fr. Mildner. He spoke excitedly. "The Spirit is at it again. Please come back to the seminary with me. I don't know what to do!"

We pulled into the S.V.D. driveway, I could hear the noise. It was Pentecost all over again. The philosophy students, the theologians as well as the gardeners and scullery maids were all responding with full voice as the spirit filled them with tongues, prophecy and ecstatic utterance. It was an "Upper Room" experience. After about two hours, the anointing lifted and things settled down. We went to our respective quarters to sleep in heavenly peace.

For many years after that Fr. Mildner sent me a card at Christmas time telling me about his boys who were now priests serving the Church in many lands around the world.

A Priests' Retreat In the Islands

The island of Romblon is part of an archipelago within the great archipelago of the Philippines. It is located a few hundred miles south of Manila. The main island is made entirely of marble. Streets of marble. Quarries of marble. Marble everywhere, none of it polished of course, except for a few ashtrays.

Each island was a distance away from the other islands. One young newly ordained priest was unfortunately assigned to an island that had a serious problem. His predecessor alienated the entire island by disrespecting a young lady. The people shunned the young priest as if he did the wrong. He was lonely and depressed. He felt like a failure. His ministry was a disaster. He came to our retreat but he was ashamed and embarrassed. He had been drinking just to get up the courage to face his brother priests.

He spent the first conference outside a window just looking in. It was very sad. At the end of the conference his brothers went outside and embraced him. He wept and accepted their love. Next day he was with us at the conferences.

The Bishop from Capiz who invited me to give the retreat to his priests asked me to make it a totally silent retreat. Imagine a band of lonely brothers coming in from their isolated island lives and asked to adhere to the monastic discipline of silence. I could not do it. I asked in prayer, "What would Jesus do?"

I arranged for a beach party with all the trimmings with music and drinks. Everybody had a great time.

While swimming in the lovely blue green waters I stepped on a very toxic sea urchin. Ouch! One of the priests took me home and the doctor came over and put me to bed with an intravenous drip to neutralize the poison. Later on when it came time to give the conference, he came back and took the needle out, propped me up and I preached the Word as best I could. This continued on till Thursday morning. What a roller coaster ride. On Friday morning the retreat was over. I ended up on my feet. Thank you, Lord! I felt better. The retreatants went back to their islands and I got ready for the trip home.

The Pastor of the parish where we had the retreat had a boat. He got me over to the Island of Tablas where there was an airport. However, there were no planes. Philippine Airlines was on strike. What to do? Manila was hundreds of miles to the north. I was tired from the retreat. I wanted to go home.

At the other end of the runway I saw a little private plane beginning to taxi towards my end for takeoff. I had my white habit on. I hoped the pilot was a Catholic. I hurried out to the place where the planes begin to rev up their engines before takeoff. I put my thumb up and made like a hitchhiker. The pilot quieted his engine and asked me where I was going. "Manila" I said." Oh! I'm sorry. I'm heading south for Bacolod", he responded. He revved up again and left us in his back wash. I was disappointed indeed. The next Philippine Airlines flight would not be here for another week.

Tablas was a very long island and to rent a boat to Panay I had to get to the opposite end. I hailed a Jeepny and after a bumpy ride to the southernmost point I got an outrigger with a Johnson engine. The boatman would take me to Panay where I could rent a car to cross the Island to get a ship to Manila.

A storm at sea

We set sail to cross the inland sea. It was beautiful. I began to relax and enjoy the ride. However, a tropical squall came up and the winds began to toss us about. The boatman had to turn into the wind lest we capsize. We were using up our gas and were going nowhere. The engine cut out. We were out of gas! We were being taken by the wind towards the South China Sea. I was frightened. I tried to pray but I couldn't. I remembered what happened in Amsterdam. So I began to pray in tongues. It kicked in and pray I did, intensely and for a long time. Finally we were blown ashore on the northern tip of Panay. We made it. We were safe. Thank you Jesus! You are good at storms!

I needed a ride into town. A pedicab (A motorized rickshaw) was in sight so I hailed him. He saw that I was an American and he quoted me a price that I knew was at least double the real fare. I had to take his terms but it made me angry. I remembered what scripture says to do in situations like this. Respond to the evil with good. God will take care of things His way. I did the right thing I' m sure. I paid the driver his fee with grace and gave him a generous tip. He looked confounded by my action. He knew that I knew he was cheating me.

In town there was an old Chevy that seemed to be held together by scotch tape and rubber bands. Could this get us to Iloilo city? God only knows. I had no other choice. The driver packed my soggy suitcase into the back and we bounced all the way across the island to Iloilo, the port city.

I went right away to the Nurses Training School of the Sisters of St. Paul de Chartres where I had given a retreat a year before. I asked for hospitality. They welcomed me and helped me to dry out. I had a nice supper and a good night sleep. Thank God for Christianity! There are believers everywhere!

Next day I got a ticket for the cargo ship to Manila but there were no cabins left. I had to sleep on the deck. It was an adventure. I think it was all part of the hundredfold. A couple of days later I pulled up in a taxi to my house. The guys asked, "how was your trip?"

Put on the Armor of God

Two ladies showed up at my door. They said they were praying and they got the word that a priest was coming to help them with the outpouring of the spirit. I was surprised for they had no way of knowing that I was home. Should I be suspicious? I was too new to all this spiritual activity to suspect anything. I had seen so much good stuff in such a short time. I was naive.

St. Peter said, "Beware the devil who goes around seeking someone to devour." Where there is true mysticism pseudo mysticism is sure to follow. Even in Medugorje there are spurious prayer groups popping up all the time. Also the devil disguises him self as an angel of light. St. Paul said, "Our fight is not against flesh and blood but against principalities and powers."

The devil accosted Jesus. He actually entered into dialogue with the evil one. Would I have to go through what he went through?

This is what happened in my case. I was leading a 40-day house of prayer experience for seven Sisters out in Lipa, about 50 miles southeast of Manila. The program was going along nicely when one day a limousine arrived owned by the lady who came to my door that day. Her written note to me was, "Please accompany the driver back to Manila to discern some prophecies that we are receiving about the "outpouring of the Spirit."

I was conflicted because of the group of Sisters that expected my leadership for the 40-day retreat. However, this situation seemed to require a response in the light of all the unusual things that were happening. There was no telephone service in that place and so I needed to check it out in person. I got in the car and we arrived back in Manila a few hours later. The lady who owned the car said that she had some prophecies addressed to my group and me. "Something big was about to break for all the believing people of Southeast Asia. It will bring about the unity of all the religions of the Orient". I was to serve this new thing, which was to be centered in Manila. There were rewards and sanctions involved for those who would serve and for those who would not serve. "For the ones who would not serve, they would walk the face of the earth till the end of time." Fear went up and down my spine.

No one taught us in the seminary how to discern the spirits. After all the good stuff I had seen over the past months how could I tell the difference between true prophecy and false.

True prophecy is the testimony of the risen Jesus in the midst of a community of believers. It is a charismatic gift given by God for the up building of the Church. St. Peter said, **"We possess the prophetic message as something altogether reliable. Keep your attention closely fixed on it as you would on a lamp shining in a dark place until the first streaks of dawn appears and the morning star rises in your hearts". (2 Peter 1:19)** Every Christian community can and should ask for it. St. Paul says, **"Set your hearts on the gift of prophecy. He who prophesies builds up the Church. The prophet speaks to men for their encouragement and their consolation." "Prophecy is for those who have faith." (1 Cor. 14)**

False prophecy, on the other hand, is the work of the devil to bring about division among the believers. It is designed to destroy communities and ruin lives. It is the pseudo mysticism that follows after true mysticism. I simply will give you the basic outline of what happened to me.

Unity in Community has been my life long desire for the Church and for myself. I was a perfect target for an enemy attack.

I was God's servant, as Job was and I was about to be tested. God permits such things and I was not exempt.

The devil is a fallen angel and is very intelligent. In fact he is super intelligent and he hates God and his servants. He figured out a way to destroy the charismatic renewal and hurt it's spokesperson. He knew the good thing that I desired and used that as his point of attack. It was my Achilles heel. My desire for unity, which energized my missionary heart. What could be better bait than a plan to bring it about?

Ten days of false prophecy followed. I was being hooked and drawn in like a fish. Everything that a missionary could desire was being promised. Day by day subtle details were creeping through and after about a week I wanted to believe what was being said. The "prophet' that was being used was proficient at channeling. I had no idea that a group of spiritists was behind all this. They would yield to unknown spirits and let them speak through their mouths. The word "Lord" was used often to make one think that this was Jesus. This paranormal or diabolical thing was coming from the realm of the spirits.

Amazing knowledge was displayed about my sister in New York. She had an invalid marriage situation with an absent spouse. For twenty years she suffered loneliness. The "Lord" declared that the whole thing could be annulled right away in this post Vatican II Church. I called my sister in New York, told her what I heard. She felt very uncomfortable with this entire unfolding drama. I was getting in deeper and deeper by the hour. Ten days went by. I was being hooked by the promise of two good things. My sister's freedom to re-marry and the promise of ecclesial unity in Asia.

But I still had an ace in the hole. The authority of the Church would be my last safe resort.

I wired Fr Harold, my boss in Mindanao. "Please come to Lipa right away. Help discern something that is beyond me." I explained a little. He was worried. He flew the 700 miles to learn what strange things were going on.

I drove back to Lipa and Harry met me there. Purissima and her friend accompanied me. Harold invited Bishop O'lalia of Lipa to help us discern this happening. The forty-day House of Prayer with the sisters was still going on in that very building.

The spirit within Purissima, the "prophetess," was being agitated by the presence of the men of God who came to help me. All of a sudden she began to scream. It seemed to be like the gospel story. "Jesus of Nazareth, what do you have to do with me? I know who you are!" I believe that the authority residing in the men of God was threatening the evil spirit within her. The screaming was like a partial deliverance. It went on for quite a while. I did not understand what was going on. No one did.

Fr. Harold and the Bishop were trying to figure out what was happening too. Neither one had ever experienced anything like this before. They thought that Purissima was having a psychotic breakdown and since I had been listening to her I must be crazy also. They suspended me on the spot and ordered me into the psychiatric ward of Makati Medical Center.

They had me observed for two weeks and then I began what seemed like house arrest at our Passionist regional house in Quezon City. This whole thing lasted over one hundred days.

One day my old friend and former assistant, Fr. Jim Lorry, C.P. came by. I asked him to do me a favor and check out this lady, Purissima. He looked her up, found her and brought her to St. Joseph's Church in Cubao. There, from the tabernacle, he saw the exorcism that dramatically took place. It was a direct action by Jesus in the Eucharist. Jim did not know what was going on and he simply related to me what he saw. Purissima looked as if she were having an epileptic fit. She was flailing her arms and legs. I believe that this took place as the demons were being cast out. After the event she was totally at peace. She herself had not known what was happening to her. Then she simply said to Fr. Jim, "Tell Fr. Owen that now I am free. He can renounce all that came from my lips".

That very day I went to see Fr. Harold. I had a purple stole and ritual in hand and asked for absolution in the external forum and renounced Satan and all evil spirits. By this action I was professing my faith in the revelation of Jesus. Harold still did not understand or believe me.

I wanted to get back to work but he transferred me to Scranton, Pennsylvania. What an inglorious way to end a beautiful foreign mission vocation!

An evaluation

A hit God sent Fr. Herb Schneider S.J. a scripture scholar, to take over the leadership of Charismatic renewal in the Philippines.

Some runs I was given a whole new dimension to my ministry. To me a new period of training in Charismatic life was given to me by the People of H.O.P.E. of New Jersey under the very able leadership of Fr. Jim Ferry. Also the sharing of life in a new Passionist charismatic community, and I even got to study spiritual psychology with the Benedictines of New Mexico. It was like a second career in Spiritual Direction using new skills that I learned from them. As Job received back double of what he lost so have I been doubly blessed in my faith walk?

More runs Through the migration of hundreds of thousands of charismatic Filipinos scattered all over the globe, the Catholic Pentecostal Movement carried the breath of the Spirit to Saudi Arabia, the Aleutians, Sweden, and Hong Kong, Australia and to many parishes in the USA and Canada. This diaspora spread the Life In the Spirit. Wherever the Filipino community settles, it seems that a Spirit led prayer group emerges. It was like the early church after Pentecost.

An error It was the devil that "planned" the crucifixion of Jesus. But the victory of the Savior of the world brought defeat to the evil one who thought he could destroy the Son of God, our Messiah. Though he intended to destroy me and the charismatic movement, at the moment, I feel like I have been saved and raised from the dead. I feel wonderfully blessed.

One night in Lipa, before all this happened, we had a very Spirit filled liturgy. Sister Jude Belmonte Paat SPC was our guest. In a sweet anointing that took place during the offertory, I was inspired to offer my life with Jesus for the Philippines. It was all in the flow of my prayer. To me it did not seem different from any other Mass.

Two years later, back home in America, I received a letter from Sister Jude. She said, that night at the Mass, she had a vision of all that I would suffer and all the spiritual consequences of my offering. The Philippines would have a religious awakening and there would even be a spiritual revolution and a change in the government. It has taken place.

"To Him whose power now at work in us can do immeasurably more than we ask or imagine, to Him be glory in the Church and in Christ Jesus, through him world without end. Amen"(Ephesians 3.20)

Phase Two

Scranton

Transitions are hard but this one was traumatic. Reputation gone, ministry gone, all seemed gone; but God was busy rearranging my life. My novititiate classmate, Fr. Isaiah Powers used to say, "I'm in sales, not in management." We sometimes have to endure "passionistic transfers" for the sake of the kingdom. All I knew, it felt like I was being brought very low. I had to trust and let go of everything.

My "Jesus only" year continued. It started when Fr. Harold and Bishop O'lalia declared my work ended. It was the dark night.

The Provincial Superior, Fr. Flavian Dougherty, at Union City, did not know what happened at Tagaytay, Lipa, Quezon City and Manila. Administratively all he could do was call on the professionals to advise him. After spending a month under observation at St. Vincent' Hospital in Harrison NY. Dr. Cassidy declared me not crazy. He said, "I was only angry at my superiors and at myself for not discerning things correctly."

It took me a long time to forgive God for He could have stepped in and enlightened me. I had a low-grade depression for four years and even though I was working again, I was under a cloud. No one understood. I felt the isolation of it all.

Brother Angelo Sena C.P. was part of the Scranton community, at that time. He was a very open fellow and even though I did not explicitly try to sell the Pentecostal movement to him, he was ready. One day we both were sitting in the priest's recreation room. It was after our noon meal. I was eating an apple and Angelo was reading the sports section of the newspaper. All of a sudden, it seemed like the heavens opened and the Spirit came down on the both of us. We responded in awe and were moved to pray in the Spirit. Angelo got the gift of tongues, and he continued to pray deeply for the rest of the afternoon. He cleaned the chapel endlessly so he could be with the Lord in the Blessed Sacrament. To this day he is still living in the anointing. Everybody sees his devotion and piety.

Many days passed and still my situation was not being resolved. I was not even allowed to minister at the prison. Weeks began to pass and I was becoming frustrated.

One morning after crying into my pillow I went to the chapel. I knelt and prayed deeply. I begged the Lord for an authentic Christian community to live in. I read John 17 to Jesus in the tabernacle and claimed the ideal of Gospel living for myself. "Father, make them one as you are in me and I am in you." Jesus' prayer to the Father has been answered for all who are willing to do what is required to appropriate it. I was certainly ready to say yes to his gift.

A week later I got a call from my Vice-Provinical, Fr. Gregory Flynn saying my written request for an official discernment had been received and a meeting would be held. I could choose a charismatic priest to represent me. Hope at last!

I asked Fr. Jim Ferry of the House of Prayer Experience to represent me at the discernment meeting. He said, "No! It would do no good". You cannot make anyone understand a thing like that. It would only muddy the waters. He asked me to come to the House of Prayer for the summer five-week program for religious men and women. I asked my Provincial if I could attend. Thankfully, he said, "Yes". Fr. Jim and the Community offered to discern my spirit and then report back to the Provincial. At the end of the program Fr. Jim and the Community affirmed my mental and spiritual health and invited me back to live with them and work with them for an indefinite period. The cloud was beginning to lift.

After my first year at H.O.P.E. I realized how much I did not know about the Charismatic Renewal and the spiritual life. But slowly, I began to fit into the spiritual culture of the place. I was becoming happy again.

However some of the more discerning members of the community noticed the deep sadness that clung to me. I had a jovial persona but it was a mask. I could not will my way out of the depression. I had been hurt too deeply for a simple quick fix. The real healing would come later in God's time and in God's unique way. For the moment I just had to be patient. Our Passionist motto needed to kick in for me, "May the Passion of Jesus be always in our hearts"!

Literally, the House of Prayer Experience was a place of hope for a lot of people. When the revival hit the U.S. some people got baptized in the Spirit but the majority of churchgoers did not. The ones who did seemed to be the odd balls since they saw everything in a whole new light. Everybody seemed to be out of sync with everybody else. A lot of people got hurt. The house of prayer became a place of refuge for the wounded charismatic minority as well as a place for the few brave souls who wanted to receive this new grace in spite of all the spiritual chaos and misunderstanding surrounding it.

Fr. Jim, Fr. Owen Sr. Maura and Sr. Gloria

At this training center many programs were given for nuns, priests and lay people. About 5,000 guests visited H.O.P.E. each year. People started to come from Australia, Europe and Lebanon.

Cardinal Suenens came in from Belgium to experience the new Charismatic community life. He started out at the dish washing machine with me. I felt very honored to be in his presence and do such lowly chores with this great churchman.

I was asked by Fr. Jim to be the Cardinal's "body guard" and get him safely back to the house through the garden after the prayer meeting. It was an interesting role I was asked to play. I enjoyed it.

One Sunday afternoon we had a big prayer meeting and about fifteen hundred people came. Werner Von Trappe was there. When he heard the many people singing in tongues together he said it was truly from God. As a musician he marveled at the point and counterpoint coming from a group that had not practiced together. Immediately he asked to be prayed over for the Baptism in the Spirit. After that he befriended our little community. The Sound of Music had touched his soul. He invited us to his dairy farm in Vermont. Three of us went to his place. Clearly this was another taste of the hundred fold.

An Amazing Bus Ride

My Paul of the Cross Province ran a three-day program on our Passionist heritage at our Monastery in West Springfield, Massachusetts. It touched me very profoundly. On the bus on the way home to the People of Hope, the Spirit came upon me. I recognized it right away this time.

Wordlessly, the Lord was communicating with me. Would I accept the wounds? My first response was no way! I kept fighting the whole idea all the way home to New York. The pressure kept building up. I could not stand it any more. This same phenomenon happened to me the first night I got back to the Philippines after my experience of the Baptism in the Spirit. My secretary had just finished praying over me when the build up of the anointing began. I thought my chest would break. I cried out "Stop! Stop!" the pressure on the rib cage let up.

Later I asked my spiritual director "What should I have done?" He said, "Never say 'stop' to the Lord but "Increase my capacity to receive you." So here on the bus I did just that and I did not say "no" though I hardly said, "yes" to His offer. It was too awesome for me to process. After this episode of wrestling with God I felt a profound peace and consolation. Later that day, as I returned to the Xavier Center at Convent Station, N.J. a prayer meeting was in progress. A member stood up and read from Luke 23. "And Jesus was nailed between two thieves". It felt like it was a confirmation of the prayer experience on the bus.

****

The Hope Community frequently embarked on campaigns called "Jesus Weeks" to promote the Catholic Pentecostal Movement. It was really a mission band to the parishes. I tagged along and heard confessions and occasionally preached. It was nice. I also learned a lot for the next phase of my life, which was coming on me soon. After three years I was invited to join the newly planned Passionist Word of the Cross Community.

Fr. Mike Salvagna was the animator of this new idea. The Passionists now had twenty-two priests and brothers in the Catholic Pentecostal Movement. Six had volunteered to be a service group for the rest. Since I was one of the six, Mike approached me and asked me to leave the inter community phenomenon of H.O.P.E. and help him and four others to begin a Passionist residence in Chelsea, New York.

On the one hand I was glad to join my own Passionist Community again but on the other I was sad to leave my newfound charismatic culture and friends.

The Word of the Cross Community

On Sept. 14, 1976, the Feast of the Holy Cross, we began our new experiment. At first we identified somewhat with the larger charismatic movement going on in the Church but after just a little while it became clear to us what God wanted of us. The charism of Paul of the Cross had to be rediscovered and relived in our day.

For six months we did no external work. Our work was to listen to the Lord and find a new lifestyle. What came forth was the plan to live together at home twelve days every month with no missions or retreats. A structure to support the contemplative dimension of our life was revealed to us.

Saint Paul of the Cross

Paul of the Cross wanted six months home and six months out. It was his rule of thumb, to which even he had to adapt. Our solution to this challenge was twelve days home and eighteen days every month dedicated to apostolic travel. We kept to this arrangement for the entire eighteen years that I was there.

The residence was a 14-room farmhouse. We had one hundred acres of land and a river view (if we trimmed our trees a bit). The Congregation bought the place in 1932 to be used as a Novitiate. Over the years it was actually used only for a mission house. Now it would take on a whole new purpose; to rediscover the lifestyle and energy of Paul Daneo.

Our first external venture was a retreat to the clergy of the New York Archdiocese. All five of us conducted this retreat as a team. It was wonderful since we all were coming forth from a contemplative home life. We could not replicate that retreat format very often because of the needs of the larger Church.

We became a band of brothers. At the end of each twelve-day retreat period separately we set out on our missions and retreats. Some of us teamed up with lay people or religious of other communities to do missions or retreats as the calls for our services came in.

Fr. Philip would do about three missions a month with Sr. Angelique O.P. Mike would go to Pittsburgh and do ecumenical television work. Malcolm would do Emmaus retreats for priests and Ben would do in-home retreats for small groups. My work at first was parish missions

Our fourteen room retreat in the woods

with a team of lay people. As time moved on we all evolved and grew with our specialized apostolates. It was very interesting to see how the Lord was leading each man differently.

Before The Word of the Cross Community got off the ground Philip had been the administrator of the Priest conventions at Steubenville, Ohio. Now at Chelsea he invited me to attend a convention with him. Two thousand priests showed up. We had a huge tent on the Campus of Holy Spirit University. The tent seemed to be symbolic of the roots of the Pentecostal meetings of the past but proved also to very practical. The priests all seemed to enjoy the setting.

At the end of the big prayer meeting we were all directed to gather into small groups to pray for specific charisms. I remembered how wonderful it was when Mrs. Yusay got healed of cancer in the Philippines. I asked for the gift of healing. All the priests in my group prayed over me. Then one priest spoke out in prophecy saying, "you have asked for the gift of healing, but it shall not be given to you. What will be given to you is the gift of love and from the overflow of that love many will be healed". To tell the truth I was a little disappointed. I wanted to be able to heal hurting people.

A week later I was at another similar type of gathering at Merton House in St. Louis, Missouri. At the end of that retreat Fr. Francis McNutt said, "now we will pray for specific gifts that you may need for your work. Please express your desire to the group. Again I asked for the gift of healing and again I got the same prophecy, this time through a Nun. "You have asked for the gift of healing but it shall not be given to you!. What you are receiving is the charism of love and from the over flow of that love many will be healed."I have never again prayed for the gift of healing. "Thank You for the charism of love, Lord!'

Around the World in 28 Days

One day Fr. Philip Bebie and I noticed an article in the Soul magazine stating that contact had been made with Chou En-lai about a possible visit of the Pilgrim Virgin to China. Our very special statue was up on the third floor of our Union City Monastery unused and under appreciated. Bishop O'Gara had purchased it in Fatima. Philip and I both knew it was destined for China. Bishop O'Gara, spent many years in prison. He was exiled from the missions in 1951. He felt that only Mary could open China to the faith.
We called John Haffert of the Blue Army in Washington, NJ and told him he could borrow the statue. He was delighted and asked us both to accompany it on the pilgrimage to China.

What an amazing grace to come our way! We'd be part of the 1982 Peace Flight that would take us around the world. A chartered 707 plane with over 200 pilgrims would be the context of our life for the next 28 days. Fatima was our first stop.

How wonderful to see where the great event of Mary's present day "visitation" took place. The Banga visitation had its origins here and thus so many blessings for so many. Part of my job was to witness about what happened when the Pilgrim

Virgin visited my mission. How happy I was to proclaim her name!

Momma Mary has visited Fatima, Lourdes, Medjugorje, Rwanda and many other places. Millions have felt loved by her touch. My own priesthood has been modally changed because of her visitation to my mission. Jesus gave Mary to us and us to Mary on Calvary. She has taken her mission very seriously. I have personally felt her love through these visits.

Israel was our next stop. It was great to see all the places that we meditated on for so many years. The highlight of my visit to the Holy Land happened on Good Friday at exactly 3 P.M. We were invited to touch the place where the Cross of Jesus stood. I placed my hand in the hole and prayed a bit and as I was pulling my hand out I cut my finger on the sharp silver marker. I began to bleed from the cut and I remember I said, "Wow!" not "ow!"

The people wanted to renew their baptisms in the Jordan. It was a great opportunity to pray for the "Baptism in the Spirit and in the Fire." Most of these folks were unaware of the Catholic Pentecostal Movement so I kept everything very low-key for these Marian pilgrims. The Spirit seemed to respect where they were at and no surprises took place. But something good did take place in each one. Of that I am certain!

Karachi and Katmandu

We flew eastward toward our next stop, Pakistan. That night we ate in a restaurant. Each of the fourteen priests that were on the flight had been entrusted with five thousand dollars in cash for the gasoline since we had no credit card for the chartered plane. I could not eat with the wallet strapped to my arm. I tucked it under my thigh. When the meal ended I forgot the wallet and walked off. A Muslim waiter came running after me. "Sir, sir you forgot your wallet." My angel was looking after me again.

Philip had the Mass at the Cathedral of St. Patrick in Kurachi, Pakistan. I had the afternoon Pilgrim Virgin service in Katmandu, Nepal. One-third of all the Catholics in Nepal showed up at my service. We all fit into one classroom. Mother Theresa's sisters came. Fr. Philip took the rest of our people around the city on a bus tour to make room for the native Nepalese in the one classroom that we borrowed from the Jesuits.

A miracle happened here. A woman from a very far village touched a handkerchief to the Pilgrim Virgin and later on touched the eyes of her blind brother. The man was healed. It was written up in a Nepalese paper, which I got to read months later.

China at last

On the train, out of Hong Kong, for Canton two days later we were busy looking at the Chinese countryside for the first time. We passed over the border into communist territory. When we reached the station at Canton the officials confiscated our precious statue and put her in a warehouse until we would leave China. We tried to convince them that we were only bringing in a work of art but they knew that there was something mysterious going on. We had our first taste of atheistic communism. It was sour indeed.

Also, they would not let us use our chartered 707. We had to fly over their air space to Beijing in their commercial plane at great expense. The whole thing about Chou En-lai was not true. We did not feel welcome at all. Beijing in 1982 was not as modern as it is today. We stayed in an old building built by the Russians many years ago in another time. We were brought to our rooms and a guard was stationed outside our door.

The next day the Chinese Tourist Bureau put us on a bus with guards assigned to watch even their own tour guides. One leader of the Red Guards harangued the tour guides right in front of us warning them of something and scolding them in advance before even the trip began.

The day trip, however, was so interesting that we began to forget the nastiness of the Red Guard. We were soon walking along the Great Wall of China. It was awesome. We saw the Terra Cotta soldiers in their ancient grave. We toured the Forbidden City and ate a 22-course Peking Duck dinner in Beijing and finally viewed a Chinese opera. It was a roller coaster of an amazing day.

Shanghai was another adventure. The priest at the Patriotic Church explained to us the situation. The Catholics in many places decided they had to adapt or die. The Church could not survive they felt unless they went along with the government. Others were more heroic. They would rather go underground, as it were, rather than compromise on even the slightest accidentals. Many went to prison for 10, 20 or 30 years. They did not trust the Patriotic Church and would not acknowledge them at all. Imagine such terrible pain and division brought on by the circumstances. As time moved on, the Wisdom of Solomon was needed to come to unity of the most minimal type. Even the leadership in Rome has been trying to help with diplomacy.

The pastor of the "Patriotic" church related to us an extraordinary thing that happened in a nearby Marian shrine Church. The Communist administration chained and padlocked the Church. The devout underground people came in the middle of the night and cut the chains and worshipped God, honored Mary and sang hymns on a special feast day in May. They recaptured the church building and every year after that on a specific secret day they would repeat their assertion of religious freedom.

On the last night in Canton we had a Mass of Intercession and thanksgiving. The Red Guards attended with guns displayed on their hips. What did we accomplish? "We labored all night and caught nothing." I think the venture cost over a million dollars to the pilgrims and the leaders of the Blue Army. We pondered the mystery and next day we picked up the Pilgrim Virgin statue at the warehouse. We headed for home, via Taiwan, Hawaii, California and Philadelphia.

Driving along route 80 in Jersey I was so tired I fell asleep at the wheel. I bounced off the center divider, I woke up and I gently moved back into my proper lane. The angels were watching over me again. Thank you, Lord!

Philip and I returned to our Word of the Cross community in Chelsea and shared for hours with Ben, Mike and Malcolm. It was an extraordinary trip. Again, how can we say thanks, Lord!

Home Sweet Home

I had seen so much! I had to process all the input of the past month. Every day I walked the woods and along the Hudson River and pondered the mystery of our global village.

When I was in South Cotabato Fr. Harold said that the Philippines were too small for me. What did he mean? Is the world my mission? Is Intercessory prayer my primary work? Time will tell!

The Friday of my 12-day home period came too soon. Though I had recuperated from the world peace flight enough to go forth again I really would have preferred to stay home and just be.

My next job was a little more local, only forty-five minutes away, and a retreat by Philip and me at the Dominican Retreat House in Sparkill, New York. It was for lay men and women. Phil and I shared the preaching and liturgies as well as the confessions and counseling sessions. At the "one on one" conferences I met Yvonne Zeller. The witness of her experience of the Passion was awesome. At age thirteen she had a locution from God that she would get polio. At age sixteen it happened. She was paralyzed from the waist down. Her parents blamed God for the polio and they became atheists. Yvonne became a Nun and a missionary to the children of the migrant workers in the Southwest. She taught school on crutches. She was part of a Franciscan community for 14 years. It was called the Sisters of Reparation of the Five Wounds of Jesus. She herself had the charism of the Passion.

At home again, The Word of the Cross Community was celebrating the feast of the Solemn Commemoration of the Passion. It was the Friday before Lent and it was a special feast day for Passionists. The five of us were deep in prayer. The song, "Were you there when they crucified my Lord?" was being played in the background. I began to feel God's presence in an unusual way. All of a sudden I was "there." It was dark but very luminous. I felt that Jesus was speaking to me about my own sorrow of being sent home from the Philippines. I still had the self pity and the low-grade depression. "You look like me," I heard. My self-pity and depression began to lift. I saw "light" and I heard, "Boast in your wounds." Others will be healed because I am touching your wounds. In that moment I "saw" the Lord glorifying my infested hurts.

Then I "heard", "It is all good news. You can tell the world. I have glorified your wounds"! It felt like the Risen Lord Jesus had actually touched my hands and my heart. Wow! What a morning!

My long winter was over at last. I had been brought very low. Now, for the first time in four years I felt good again. I no longer had to fake it. "My soul magnifies the Lord! God has done great things for me and Holy is His Name!"

Was this latest experience connected to my theophany on the bus? The wounds were already there. They just needed to be healed and "glorified." As I write this little book I am connecting the dots and things that never made sense to me are now becoming full of meaning. Psychologists would call this a "therapeutic narrative." We might just call it an anointed review of life.

Our home time continued happily for about ten more days. We invested in a Franklin stove. We had plenty of firewood on our land. All we had to do was gather it. It was very nice indeed!

A true ghost story

Fr. Mike Salvagna and I were invited to preach a mission in a town in the hills of Pennsylvania. It was near Shenandoah. A young woman from Philadelphia joined the team to help us to pray for healing. She stayed for the week in a private home. The matriarch of the family had recently died. In life she ran the family catering business and was a control freak. Her son asked for prayers for his mother. She was causing some disturbance in the house. The young woman, Sharon, was given her bed to sleep in. It was 2:00 A.M.. The restless spirit of the mother came back into the room and all hell broke loose. The dog pooped on the floor. The girl sat bolt right up in the bed. The atmosphere was like ice.

The following night was the healing service at the mission. The son of the restless lady had asked for special prayers for his mother so she could rest in peace. We all went into the dining room of the rectory. The young woman, Sharon, volunteered to be prayed over in proxy for the deceased mother. We foolishly consented and the prayers began. Suddenly the young lady slipped into a trance and the voice of the matriarch came forth from her mouth. Obviously she had issues with her family and needed to deal with some unfinished business. She spoke for almost twenty minutes. We did not know how to stop her. I asked Fr. Mike to pray deliverance over her. He did and the young lady came back to her normal self. Wow! What an experience.

The son said that it was definitely his mother speaking. The girl did not know what was going on. She had no memory of the trance.

The next day as we were leaving,we asked the Pastor to say a special Mass for the mother in her bedroom. I trust he did.

Priests are very often asked to bless a house. Sometimes it's just a good thing to do, like for new homeowners. But sometimes it's because the house is haunted. I believe that discarnate spirits (ghosts) exist and very often they need help. A Mass for the repose of their souls is frequently the only answer.

Every night, we of the Word of the Cross Community would gather around the fireplace and share our faith or discuss things that had to do with our life together. I had never experienced community like this before. Before this, it was the intimacy that was missing.

Intimacy is the therapeutic answer to the anonymous lifestyle of the traveling preacher. We were discovering the value of the six months "in" and the six months "out" rule of thumb of Paul of the Cross. There were many other things we discovered as we had Ben Kelley facilitate Paulacrucian charism meetings regularly by the fireplace.

Fellowship of the Beloved Disciple

Later on, I ventured into a program called "Castellazo", that attempted to mediate the charism of Paul Daneo. It was popular and successful in South America. When I adapted it for my own, I used a lot of the things that I learned from Ben and the men at Chelsea. It was like a Life in the Spirit program for Passionists. I led three of these programs but the idea did not catch on with our North American Passionists so I let it go.

The home times were very happy times indeed and went by very fast. Several years of months passed by in the pleasant apostolic rhythm of our lifestyle.

Gethsemane on the Hudson Retreat was our next venue for our apostolic time. A Retreat for lay people again. One of my other brothers was with me this time and Yvonne was there again. The days passed quickly and at our closing liturgy on Sunday a phenomenal thing happened. At Communion time I was walking toward Yvonne to give her the host. The "breath of God" seemed to come forth from the host and Yvonne went down under its power. She rested in the Spirit for a time and then the Mass continued. The final blessing came and I knew I had to talk with Yvonne about what she experienced during that ecstatic moment. It was a mystical moment with the Lord and she felt peace. I felt the Spirit too and I suspected that we were being drawn to work together in the mission.

That summer I went to Chicago to study at the Word of God Institute. I was also praying hard about this apparent leading of the Spirit with Yvonne. In no way did I want to be deceived again by my own interpretation of what I thought was happening.

I delayed for as long as I could. I think I was afraid also of dealing with Yvonne's polio in an ongoing way. If I accepted Yvonne as a partner in mission I would also have to accept her polio. To me she was really a "crucified one of today". We definitely had to talk and pray some more.

Labor Day in the Bronx Botanical Garden was the time and place for our discernment meeting. It turned out to be a very pleasant experience and all fear left me. We would work together and even be friends.

Our first apostolic venture was to be a workshop on the meaning of suffering. It was 1980, the United Nations Year of the Handicapped. We gathered a team of four, a blind girl who played the guitar, an accident victim in chronic pain, Yvonne on crutches and me with my now "glorified" wounds.

We were invited to speak at a prayer meeting in Bellerose, L.I. Yvonne was petrified. She never spoke in public before except to the children on the missions in California. She took a tranquilizer and did O.K. with plenty of room for improvement. The people accepted us and our message. We called it logo therapy (man's search for spiritual meaning). Thus was the beginning of a ministry with Yvonne that has lasted for 35 years.

The contemplative life presumes an active life, at least according to Fr. Richard Rohr, O.F.M. I agree with his insight and so the Word of the Cross Community's lifestyle is very valid and comfortable for me. For example the trip to China was an example of active ministry. My contemplative period afterward was one of processing the great event. Conversely, after a good period of prayer and silence at home I needed to go forth and preach again about what I contemplated during time at home. St Thomas writes that preaching is the handing over to others that which has been contemplated. It seems that if we are faithful to the contemplative life, the well will never run dry.

Every year I tried to make a workshop of some kind to stay current with theology, missiology or psychology. Yvonne wanted to make the six-week program at the Benedictine Monastery at Pecos, NM. At first I said, "yes, I'd like to make that program too." She was happy about having someone along for companionship and to help with her luggage. However, later I began to have some second thoughts, I had all I wanted of the Charismatic workshops and told her I decided I would not go. She was very disappointed for she knew she could not travel alone. After a little bit of pondering I changed my mind and said I'd go "to manage her bags and push her wheelchair." What a divine set-up it turned out to be!

Abbot David Gaeretz, O.S.B., one of the discoverers of the new relationship of psychology and charismatic spirituality created a six-week program to help priests, nuns and laypeople experience this new gift for the Church. I realize now that I was searching for this dimension for years but did not know it. It was a continuous explosion of "Aha!" moments that were going off in my soul every day during this program. After four weeks I returned to Chelsea to continue with a reading program for a year. It was great. I could not wait to get busy preaching about my new discoveries. I thought that this possibly is to be my second "career."

The year did go by quickly with a few little workshops attempted for some friends. Yvonne and I were surprised at our return to Pecos that we understood so much. It was our experience in the field over the years that helped us so much to understand "everything." The final two weeks of the course affirmed our understanding and encouraged us for this new emphasis. We had the knowledge but we needed the words to articulate what we knew connaturally. Wow, God! This is exciting!

We were flying home to New York with a priest friend who took the program with us and he did not see anything that we saw. He was not thrilled at all. It was just another workshop to him. What was all this insight telling us about our future work?

Home Again to the Word of the Cross Community

The autumn mission season was approaching. September 14, the Feast of the Exaltation of the

Cross is always very special for me. God has touched my life and His cause is my cause.

"May I never boast of anything, but the cross of our Lord Jesus Christ. Through it, the world has been crucified to me and I to the world" (Gal. 6: 14)

Man's search for meaning is such a strong movement of the soul. I must have understanding of everything that pertains to my salvation and spiritual life. In a little while it will be eternity. There is an urgency to know and to understand.

My community is a great source of knowledge and consolation. John Paul the Great said that heaven is not so much a place as it is a state of soul. Our heaven is now and our eternal life has already begun. I am fortunate to have a heavenly home on earth. It is a safe place to live. We have agreed on a lifestyle that puts Jesus right in the center of everything. We are not angels but we try to be repentant men of God who are intent on ongoing conversion and spiritual growth. I am a beneficiary of the legacy of Paul of the Cross.

Inner Work

I have started to write down my dreams so I can monitor what is going on in my soul. Up until now, the overt external world, my emotions and actual graces were all I focused on. I did learn a little about journaling at the Kresge House of Prayer but it was not the same as working with my dreams.

We organized all the most important stuff that we learned and we put it into workshop form. Yvonne and I got invited to do a summer dream program at Fr. John Bertolucci's House of Prayer in Little Falls, NY. It was fun but exhausting. On the way home on the Thruway we stopped at a roadside picnic table to have Mass. After communion we heard a prophetic word. "You have put your act together, now take it on the road." We could not help but laugh at the words we heard.

We did have something good to offer the Church. Abbot David now had two disciples who were itinerant teachers. When we saw him next we excitedly told what was happening. He was delighted. We continued doing these "Kingdom Within" retreats all over the Eastern seaboard. Finally people kept wanting more so we developed phase two of the Kingdom Within series and then later phase three and even phases nine and ten. A wonderful bi-product of these sequential retreats was that a Community was developing because to make any one of the retreats you had to have taken the previous phase. It was a natural screening program. It vetted out the ones who were not serious about the whole idea of community.

Finally we had a weekend program called the introduction to the "Community of the Beloved disciple." It was based on Fr. Ray Brown's book about the early Church and the theology of the Beloved disciple in Ephesus. It went over very well. The people liked it and even wanted to "join" it.

The original community at Ephesus disappeared after St. John the Apostle died. It had high Christology and high "anima." Women were respected and revered. They had a very high place in the society unlike the other faith communities that grew up around St. Matthew, St. Luke and St. Mark. Some say that the Blessed Virgin Mary whom the beloved disciple took "unto his own" was in that community until such time as she was assumed into heaven.

The people on our retreats all agreed that the community should never have disappeared. It should be started up again. Twenty-eight people signed up and made a commitment to become "one" and to become the answer to Jesus' prayer and that we **become one as the Father and I are one." (John 17:21).**

****

Back at the "ranch" in Chelsea we were about to experience our first communal loss. One of the priests in the group, Fr. Malcolm Cornwell, felt we were too far off the beaten path and our solitude was more than he could handle. He missed the larger Congregation. We had grown into a house of prayer with a very rarified atmosphere. We wished him well and blessed him for the rest of his unique journey. A year or so later he was elected Rector of our Hartford monastery. We were very happy for him though his leaving was a great loss to us.

****

After the second half of our training program at Pecos we moved on to Einsiedeln, Switzerland. The program consisted of lectures by some of the best Jungian Analysts and Psychiatrists in Europe. Each man would teach for a half day on the material that had become his forte. Two great people every day for two weeks. Also, every day we would have professionals from the Jungian center in Kusnacht and from the Pecos staff available to do our dreams with us or just talk as we were led.

Phase Three

Spiritual Growth

At this point in our story let me digress. When I was in the missions I had a problem. Either I would be too much for my listeners or not enough. The spiritual life is not lived out in a vacuum. There are real people involved in everyone's story and people progress at different speeds.

Seven Levels of Faith

I wish I knew about these levels early on in my ministry. Msgr. Chester Michael of Arlington, VA did some great research on this subject and the people of the Baltimore area learned it and taught me about it. It was a real "Aha!" moment for me and answered a lot of questions about some apparent failures I experienced in my ministry.

The problem is that the people on any given level do not believe that the level above them even exists. They can't see it and they can't even hear of it. "Having eyes they see not. Having ears they hear not." It is too threatening.

We are all called on by God to grow and grow until the day comes when we are mature in the faith and in love. Lord, bring to completion the work that you have begun in us!

When I was 22 I read Edmund Burke's life of Paul of the Cross. I was impressed by the many experiences of God that Paul had. I think I joined the Passionists for that very reason. I wanted to experience God like Paul experienced Him.

We hold a treasure in earthen vessels

Two anecdotes tell a lot about me. First, the Avis commercial proclaims, "When you are second best you try harder." That's me. I preached so hard my vocal chords gave out. The doctor said, "You have market vendors disease" Surprised and taken aback I asked, "What is that?" "You have pink vocal chords from talking too long and too loud," he replied. What shall I do", I asked. "Shut up," he advised. "I can't. I talk for a living". I ended up taking voice lessons and tried to preach less intensely.

Anecdote #2. When I was a college boy I used to run cross-country. One day at Van Cortland Park in the Bronx at the N.Y.U. meet there were 640 runners in the race. The gun went off and I gave it all I had. In the middle of the race there was a log jam on the trail. I could not pass anyone. Ahead I noticed a briar patch. I went through it. I legitimately passed about a hundred runners but when I emerged my legs were covered with blood.

For me, at that time, it was worth it. Maybe I am competitive. I guess I do try harder. It all might go back to surviving poverty in Queens Village. I think this kind of thing is the root of our shadows.

Bali Hai Is Calling!

John Haffert of the Blue Army called again. Would you like to try China again? A rich Chinese businessman heard about our plight. He said he could get us in to southern China through Macao, a Portuguese colony.

Also the Pacific Islands were in need of a "visitation." The mystery of the Visitation is deep and continues on in time. Mary visited her cousin in Ain Karim and then later on to us at Lourdes, Fatima, Rwanda, Medjugorje and now through the Pilgrim Virgin statue pilgrimages to the various countries of the world.

This latest invitation sounded wonderful because I could get to see my beloved Philippines again. It seemed right that we go.

This time we headed from east to west. We took off from Philadelphia again. This time I made a reservation at the Marriott Hotel so I could sleep for a whole day when we got back. I wanted no more surprises on Route 80.

We stopped at Guadalupe to ask Our Lady for a safe trip. We made one more stop in Acapulco to pick up water for our plane. Montezuma would have his revenge. Many had diarrhea all the way to Tahiti and beyond; Fiji, Samoa, New Guinea and the Philippines as well. Imagine, we drank Mexican water all across the Southern Ocean!

Tahiti was great. Samoa and Fiji, too. Bishop Pearce, chief chaplain of the flight, had been the bishop of these islands. The natives had been notified of their bishop's return and they went bonkers. What a reception they had ready for him. It was fantastic. Thank you, Lord, for inviting me to the party!

One of the Fijians read an article in Soul Magazine about the happening in Banga and he asked me if I was the priest who did not have time for the Blessed Mother when she came to Mindanao? My infamy preceded me to the South Seas. I had to admit my guilt.

Port Moresby, New Guinea was very interesting. It seemed like the modern world passed it by. Of all the missions in the world it seemed the most challenging. Very high mountains, the lack of roads, an incredible number of languages and cultures that changed with every mountain range. I was embarrassed to think that I said to Fr. Ernest Hotz that I thought that the Philippines was the most difficult of all the missions.

Next stop, the Pearl of the Orient the Philippines! It had been ten years since I was exiled and I longed to see my first mission again. Before we landed I had asked the people to give a gift to my favorite charity in Manila. An orphanage for handicapped children run by the Holy Spirit Sisters. This saved them from having to give to some dubious beggars on the street. The passengers donated $2,500. The night before we arrived the orphanage suffered a robbery. Their $2,500 payroll had been stolen. They were overwhelmed when out of the blue, literally, the money came home to them.

The Filipinos really know how to do a sacred welcoming. Two million people showed up at the airport and along the route to the city and finally at the Luneta where the Mass was to be said. In the crowds I even saw Mother Madeline, who gave me my first preaching job after my exile from Mindanao. I saw Fr. Ed Deviny C.P., who had taken over for me in Banga, He was there to greet the Pilgrim Virgin. Cardinal Jaime Sin said the Mass and Bishop George Pearce preached. It was wonderful to behold.

I wanted to stay but we only were to be in the Philippines for 22 hours. The next morning we were on the road again for China.

Hong Kong was as modern as New Guinea was primitive. The hotels were beautiful. The stores were like a wonderland. It is awesome to see what the people of the world can do for business and commerce.

The next day was interesting. We sailed to Macao in a Hovercraft. A tour bus then took us on the next phase of our journey. The wealthy man that arranged the trip talked to the Red Guard at the Border. It went very smoothly. No problem getting the Pilgrim Virgin through this time.

The trip into the interior was uneventful. Finally we entered the driveway of an Inn. We sat down for a very nice meal. There were no Christians to receive the Statue. We enthroned the Pilgrim Virgin on a table and that was it. No ceremonies or speeches. Just a confused wait staff. They were Buddhists, Taoists and Animists brainwashed by Communist ideologues. One girl seemed to have some faith. She made the sign of the Cross. It was all that China could give at that moment.

Next day we moved on to Southeast Asia. We flew over Vietnam, Laos, Cambodia and Burma. Finally we landed in Calcutta, the home base of Mother Theresa.

India is a land of intense religious belief and practice. Most of the people are Hindus. In fact, at our gatherings the next day most of the people who attended our services were Hindu. The Catholics though seemed to be very bright and faithful. They were a minority in a culture that was very different though not hostile as was China. In Calcutta we visited the House of Mother Teresa's sisters. It was very impressive in its simplicity.

New Delhi was different than Calcutta. It also had its challenges, like every city of the world. From there we went by bus to see the Taj Mahal. It is all it's cracked up to be.

Getting out of Delhi was not as easy as getting into it. The dispatcher would not give us clearance to take off until we gave him a gift. For about five hours the two hundred of us sat in the waiting room. We did not want to give money but eventually at almost midnight the pilots decided to give him a few bottles of whiskey. He was satisfied. We could continue our journey.

Egypt was an all-night flight away. It was our gateway to the Holy Land. We were there just two years earlier but that was with a whole different group of pilgrims. I was beginning to feel at home in Israel. It was becoming my central point of reference. Jerusalem is a place of which you can't get enough. The mysteries that took place there are infinitely knowable and boundlessly understandable. You can't say that about too many other places in the world.

Then on to Rome. The Eternal City was also a familiar place to me. How strange it is that a little kid from Queens Village, an insurance salesman from New York Life, would become so well traveled. I am very grateful to God for it all. I have learned so much by visiting so many countries. In my room I put pins on a map and I needed 56 pins to tell the story. Again I say, thank you, Lord!

****

Driving north on Route 80 felt comfortable. This time I was working off a good night's sleep. I was glad to be home in America again! I remember the first time I got home from the Orient after a long time away. I kissed the ground. It was absolutely sincere and spontaneous. I may be a traveling salesman for God but I am an American who loves to come home.

Hometown U.S.A. for me was Fishkill, NY. There was a main street and we did our food shopping there, our banking as well. Chelsea was three miles away. It was only a hamlet along the Hudson. The only thing you could buy there was a postage stamp. I loved it. I am a New York City boy but rural life agrees with me. Banga was really rural and I loved it as well.

Me, Vince, Ben & Mike

We lost another member of the Word of the Cross Community. Philip was suffering from something mysterious. He decided that Hartford would be better for him and he left us. He was very gifted and his moving on was a great loss. A year later he died of cancer.

Mike too felt the need to leave us. His mom was alone in Pittsburgh and there was television work he could do there. Vince had gone to another mission house in Florida. What was going on? Ben and I were now a community of two and he was getting sick a lot of the time from bronchiectasis, shingles, etc. I was becoming his caregiver. We had no employees. But it was still a life-giving situation. I was now cook, maintenance man, infirmarian and missionary.

The Provincial notified us that he and the consulters were selling our property and it looked like the end was near.

In the scriptures Jesus gave us the word that two or three was enough and both Ben and I desired to continue on. We drove all over trying to find a house to rent but we realized there was nothing we could afford. Finally the man who was buying our property was willing to let us stay on. It was a solution for him as well. For $750 per month we could pay his taxes. He was not ready to subdivide and build. He was contented and we were able to buy some time. The house had fourteen rooms and one hundred acres of land.

We continued our complete monastic horarium with just the two of us. It was a bit thin but it was real and we were happy. It proved to me that to have authentic community you did not need to have big numbers. Jesus plus two is the Christian quorum.

Creative Chaos

Yvonne and I got an invitation to give a retreat to a Religious Community in the South. It was a much-evolved group and we thought we could use some of the more subtle tools in our kit bag.

One of the things that we had branched out into were the methods of M. Scott Peck M.D. to confect authentic community by working the community through the archetypal stages of pseudo community, creative chaos, emptiness, and finally to authentic community. It really works if everything goes right in the group.

My Partner in Mission

The first four days of our retreat went very well. One Sister said of the traditional conferences that it was the best retreat she'd made in 20 years.

Now, we thought was the time to bring the folks to what we thought was their next step. At this point we bombed out.

Self-revelation and confrontation were the standard tools needed to bring about the unity.

The retreatants had not asked for this dynamic and some resisted and even walked out. What started out to be a wonderful victory for us turned out to be a debacle. The superior, who blessed us with his trust, did not know what to do to save the day. At the conclusion, I believe he was glad to see us go.

The shadow

Dealing with the shadow was our problem. We all have our shadows that still very often subliminally rule our behaviors. That is why we prefer to live in anonymity. But anonymity is public enemy #one of our goal; authentic community.

I have a friend from the Congo who had a pet gorilla in his house. His name was Sebastian, he was tame and gentle and my friend felt comfortable living with him. The day came however when it was deemed best that the gorilla moves on to his next step at the animal sanctuary and then on to his natural home in the wild.

It is O.K. to live with and make friends with our inner gorilla for a time, but the day must come to bring the emerging monster into the free air of the overt world.

At the retreat we probably went beyond our job description. We were not called to handle the shadow sides of a lot of very good people. Shadows are those parts of our personality that are not in our consciousness. They are dangerous if allowed to come to full growth. This is where inner work comes in.

Well, our retreat in the South may or may not have been a complete disaster. I'll find out when I meet God face to face. Most likely it was an occasion for me to learn some humility.

Fr. Richard Rohr said in his book "Falling Upward" that he prayed to have at least one humiliation a day for his growth. I have not prayed for humiliations, but they come regularly anyway.

The thorn in the flesh that St. Paul talks about was a gift from God to keep him from getting puffed up. He had been lifted up to mystical states and the heady experiences of his prayer life needed to be balanced out by a few trials. God has blessed me with an anointed prayer life and with a few trials too. Thank You God!

****

Home time with Ben was quite different. After 14 years I had come to know a lot of what he knew. I knew all his stories and he knew mine. However we still did O.K. because our prayer life was always current and fresh. Charismatic prayer is never rote or boring. We went along fairly well for a few more years. The work for him was mostly writing. He wrote three books while at Chelsea. "Spiritual Direction According to Paul of the Cross," "Listen to His Love," and a book for children. He also did spiritual direction and "in home" retreats for small groups. I mention this because Ben kept us going financially. His royalties and stipends paid most of the rent.

Yugoslavia

An old friend of mine was taking a group of friends to Medjugorje, in Croatia. I was asked to give a retreat to the group. It was fun and exciting to visit the site and venue of Mary's ongoing current visitation. We (Yvonne and I) met the visionaries and were even present when Mary showed up to talk to them. We were about ten feet away from the spot where Mary apparently was during this wonderful visit. When Mary appeared, the visionaries became ecstatic. What a grace for them and for us to see them in that blessed moment.

At St. Joseph's church, in Medugorje, visiting priests were given the honor of taking turns preaching from the pulpit. I got Sunday, our final day. I loved it. What a privilege! Thanks, Lord!

The flight home was hard on Yvonne's legs. Her circulation was poor. The women took turns in massaging her legs during the flight home.

The Home Stretch

My life together with Ben was not perfect but it was better than some other communities that seemed to have "everything" going for them. I think I am addicted to authenticity. Ben was a man definitely consecrated to the truth. We got along very well because of this shared value.

Ben was growing weaker by the month. I had to plan my missions around his needs. I lined up my work so that I could always cook his supper, drive within a one-hour radius and get home in time to check up on him before he retired. It all went well for a while, until one night I got home and found out that he had collapsed on the floor. His Partner in Mission was Jeanne Wilson of Middletown, CT.

She called and he did not answer the phone. Jeanne immediately called our volunteer fire dept. and had them check on Ben. The door was locked and Ben was inside on the floor. They opened things up and ministered to him. When I got home the excitement was all over. I knew then that the Word of the Cross Community was over too.

When Ben got out of the hospital he was assigned to the infirmary in Hartford. I was now a hermit. What do I do now? Where do I go? A friend of mine offered to pay the rent. This continued for three months. The Provincial, Fr. Robert Joerger, told me to find a monastery or Passionist residence to live in. He said, "We don't do hermit."

I started out here in Jamaica and I'll probably end up here. The monastery was dedicated the same year I was born. It has been a blessing to me my whole life. When I was a teenager I remember coming here for visits. In College I definitely remember a lot of visits. A prayer life was begun here.

Immaculate Conception Monastery

My first retreat was made here. Before we could graduate from St. Francis College we had to make a weekend retreat. My work schedule conflicted with the scheduled class retreat date so I asked to make mine the following weekend. It was a fortuitous happening. Retreats for college boys are usually very unruly. My retreat was with a group of old timers who loved silence. My roommate, a venerable old guy, said, "Young man, let us kneel and pray. Let's keep silence until Sunday afternoon." We prayed for this and we were truly anointed for this sacred time. I remember being alone in the garden. I felt the Holy Spirit come over me for the first time in my
life. It spoiled me for all lesser things.

I was selling Insurance at the time so I decided to organize a retreat group from the New York Life Insurance Co. I was not a very successful promoter because I was incredibly shy and insecure but I meant well. However, it got me identified with a movement in the Church, "the Retreat Movement". Ever since, everything I have ever done has been connected with some movement or other. Fr. Jim Ferry used to say, "Look to see where the Spirit is moving, then affirm what's happening by helping it to happen."

I continued to make retreats and finally realized that God was calling me to serve Him full time. I applied to the Passionists. They accepted me. The rest is history.

In 1995, after Ben was safely relocated at our Hartford house. I had to find my own new home. Fr. Justin Kerber invited me to live in Jamaica. 'Mi casa, su casa,' he said. Thank You, Justin!

I felt very comfortable because of this welcoming phrase. My house is your house! It was so sincere on his part. It was a healing moment.

There is one thing about being on the mission band. It is very easy to adapt one's ministry to a new Community. Yvonne was still part of my team and we continued with the Kingdom Within retreats. However, I had no prayer meeting going on at any local situation.

The Public Chapel was being renovated but was not ready for use yet. We began a little group in the Retreat House and slowly the people began to come.

Meanwhile every month we went down to Philadelphia to attend the very big prayer meeting of Msgr. Vince Walsh. Something new was going on. We continued to seek God's face through this new movement. It was called "Revival". It seemed to be a "Renewal" of the Renewal.

The Charismatic Renewal in the Catholic Church started in 1967 at the Arc and the Dove retreat house with a group from Duquesne University. It went from there to Ann Arbor. MI and then on to Detroit where I experienced it in 1971. It brought many blessings to many people but now it seemed to be waning as a movement. God is Almighty and never gets tired but we do! Anyway, Yvonne and I pursued this new action of the Holy Spirit. Every month we drove down to Philadelphia and appropriated the new graces being poured on Presentation B.V.M. parish and the Catholics of that area. Our new little prayer group in Jamaica picked right up on it as we learned how to praise God in a whole new way. It was an important step in our development.

We Love a Party

At this point a big decision was being made for me, a shift from being on the road or staying home to pastor an emerging community. One element of my grace name is community builder and that helped me to say yes to the transition.

The Grace Name

In 1977, I made a directed retreat under the Jesuits at Wernersville, Pa. It was another life changer. Among other things, they taught me about the name that God calls me.

Before we were conceived God knew us. He had a specific mission for us to fulfill, and the mission is described in our name. For example Jesus is the one who saves. His name is his mission. Also the whole litany that flows from that quintessential part of His name tells more about Him.

We all have our grace name and a litany of descriptive elements to it. Mary's litany describes her mission and from the very synthesis of titles is her name, Mary.

My name is John, beloved disciple. Son of Mary, brother of Paul of the Cross, preacher of the Word, man of vision, community builder.

St Joseph, Paul, Therese and all the saints and **you** have a Grace name. It behooves all of us to experience this reality.

It is revealed in prayer. It is like a big insight or prophecy. It is an "Aha" moment that changes one's life. Once I experienced my name I introduced people to the process of learning their names. Hundreds of people now have experienced their mission, their name.

"Other sheep I have that are not of this fold; them also I must bring."

That first summer we had time to do some experiential "Research in the Glory." We took one whole month to visit some communities of other traditions to see what the Spirit was doing with them.

Pensacola, Florida had the most impressive Revival happening going on. It was in Brownsville, Assembly of God Church. Every day, six days a week starting at 6 A.M. people began lining up to get in at 6 P.M. The service started at 7 P.M. Six thousand people racing for 3,000 seats. The pastor had to build an annex with closed circuit TV to seat the extra 3,000 people.

They had to build an enormous parking lot with security guards. They bought several blocks of houses and tore them down. The regular members of the church had to consent to all this for the sake of this unexpected Miracle of Grace.

It all began when a traveling evangelist, Rev. Steve Hill came to do a Sunday service for his friend, Pastor John Kilpatrick. In the middle of the service the Holy Spirit came down and held the people in thrall and ecstasy for many hours. The next day the same thing happened and everyday for about five years. Over three hundred thousand people were baptized in the Spirit and Fire. Yvonne and I attended for five nights and we were amazed with what God was doing. As members of a different tradition, we were in awe and envious. It was good of God to do what He was doing for our Protestant brethren. I prayed that this would happen in the Catholic Church as well. I could easily visualize people coming up by the thousands to the Monastery from the subway on Hillside Avenue. Lord, do it for us, please! We need Revival too.

Another significant place was the Calvary Summer Camp meeting in Ashland, VA. Rev. Ruth Ward Heflin was the pastor. She was a very holy woman. She had preached the gospel in every country of the world. Even in North Korea, Siberia, Central Asia, Nepal and other difficult places. She preached mightily every day and night. Gold dust literally came down on the listeners. The people experienced fillings turning to gold. Two of my crowns were changed from white to gold. I was dumfounded. Many healings and miracles happened at her meetings. Most nights the meetings did not break up till after midnight.

Msgr. Walsh of Presentation Parish in Philadelphia had several revival meetings daily. At some meetings the numbers reached 1,000. Holy laughter seemed to be a common manifestation here. This is where the people of Jamaica came to experience Revival in a Catholic setting. The Presentation prayer meeting has since ceased to exist and Msgr. Walsh is now serving in another parish. At the time of this writing the only Catholic Revival meeting left is at our place in Jamaica, NY. "The Spirit blows where it wills."

Vita Consecrata

The consecrated life is for those who are called to it. It usually entails living single for the Lord. Several vows are characteristic to this lifestyle. Also a definite culture emerges as the called members work out the elements of their particular charism.

As for me, God called me to be a follower of St. Paul of the Cross. I am a Passionist. We take the vows of poverty, chastity, obedience and the vow to promote devotion to the Passion of Our Lord.

While I was at Chelsea, NY some of us articulated the vows in a new way for ourselves. It goes like this: "I vow to be generous with all I have. I vow to be single for the Lord and live a universal love. I vow obedience to the Holy Spirit of truth in all things and I vow patience in all circumstances."

It's not that we were trying to be holier than other consecrated people but it makes more sense to us than the old formula.

ST. PAUL OF THE CROSS
Founder of the Passionists

For myself I witness that my assets in life are my time, treasure and talents. I try to be generous with these gifts as best I can. When I was a subdeacon in Scranton, our director, Fr. Harold Reusch allowed us to stay up an extra hour at night. I decided to pray the stations each night without using prayers or formulas. After doing this for a couple of months I vividly realized that Christ emptied Himself for me. Therefore I should empty myself for others.

At that time our Philippine mission was just opening up and the kenosis of Jesus began to speak to me. I could empty my self of my language, my culture, my temperate climate, my family and everything else I could think of. The Philippines was my answer. It would do all those things for me. My call to a specific mission was being made clear.

I was not being called to the West Indies, it seemed, because the language was still English and the Island country was very near. The missionaries in Jamaica got home on furlough every year. The kenosis, the self-emptying love of Jesus, is what I sought. Generosity and kenosis was to be my translation of poverty.

Right or wrong I thought the Spirit was leading me, during these nightly prayers. Later I found out that Jamaica was probably a much tougher mission than the Philippines because of the variety of religions, violence and many other factors.

Universal love was another thing altogether. This precluded spousal love and all that that entails. I grew up with three beautiful sisters and a lovely Mom. I love women and am very comfortable with them. To be without them is unthinkable for me. I just simply must learn to love them all if I am to succeed. I try my best to be ever inclusive. The charism of celibacy, I believe has made me unmarriageable.

Obedience to the Pope, Bishop and to the superior did not seem to be specific enough. The Holy Spirit was very busy with me all day long. How was I to think of all His nudges and lights. Must I not be faithful to every grace? I have accepted this as my challenge over the years. It did not make me scrupulous or crazy. It was more of a dialogue of lovers always desirous of doing the other's will. God has been very gentle with me, even though my story may seem otherwise.

To me the Passionist sign over my heart symbolizes patience. I had to practice a lot of it in the missions, in my human relationships, in all my works of compassion and especially in trying to keep my vows.

Some Surprises of the Spirit

Consecrated life is filled with surprises. Regularity and fidelity to the vows is just part of the life. The surprises of the Holy Spirit are a huge part too.

Quadruple Bypass.

Dr. Heffer, my cardiologist looked at me with an unusual look in his eye. My Stress test showed a huge blockage in my arteries. The surgeon, Wilson Ko M.D., did a wonderful job of extending my life. That was in 2,000 A.D.

Several years later, Dr. Gustafson, after putting in two stents, asked me to stay overnight for observation. At supper I choked on a chicken sandwich. A major hemorrhage followed. I was bleeding out. Some of the doctors were willing to let me go. I was an old man now and it was late and everything was shut down and above all they did not know what they were dealing with. Some thought it was the stents that had just been put in. Dr. Gustafson insisted that they do a CT scan and pin point the problem. The test showed Borhaave's Syndrome. A tear in the Esophagus down between the stomach and the diaphragm. The mortality rate for this syndrome was 100%, unless surgery by a very skilled surgeon intervened almost immediately

Dr. Paul Lee was just sitting down to dinner when his beeper went off. He responded immediately and four hours later I was in the recovery room. He saved my life. Thank you, God and Dr. Lee. I choose life.

The Stroke

I was at Mass and had just received Holy Communion. I felt a bit lightheaded and dizzy. I struggled to get to my chair. I plopped down feeling a bit drunk. This time it was physical. After breakfast, the Rector, Fr. Peter Grace insisted that I check it out. We called an ambulance and the triage team diagnosed it as a stroke. It felt like the end of my life, as I knew it.

I felt like a rag doll. The core of my body would not obey me. It has been a huge change but I did not feel too bad because I have lived a full life and maybe it's time to begin this next phase of my life.

My longtime doctor and friend, Gregory Gustafson visited me in my room. He said, rehab, rehab, rehab. It's been almost three years since that day and it was true there is no cure for a stroke except rehab. "Muscle memory" is what I had to work on, day in and day out if I wanted to walk again. At the time of this writing I am doing fine with a four wheeled walker called a Rolator. When I wake up I feel no pain and I have to remind myself that I can't walk, lest I fall on my face when I get up.

Lability is one of the consequences of a stroke. It is like when the gear of a car slips from first gear to third. Tears happen at the most embarrassing times. Probably we all cry at one time or another. In some cultures it is very common for men to cry. In Ireland some men have what is called the Irish blather. They can cry over certain ballads and sad political happenings in their history. I am Irish plus I have lability from the stroke but sometimes I have what is called the gift of tears.

Fr. Steve and me in our wheel chairs.

We both had Strokes

This is compared by some to a second baptism. In Banga I got it when the Pilgrim Virgin came by and several other times in my story. Also at my Cursillo graduation. These moments were life changing. I respond to anything that is archetypal or transcendental. Anything heroic or noble, the beautiful things in our humanity. It all touches me and brings me to tears. It is more of a blessing than a curse. It is what it is.

Justin goes home

They notified me that Justin Garvey was dying. The community members took turns doing vigil with him in the cardiac section of Mary Immaculate Hospital. I wanted to be with Justin when he died. I volunteered for the 11 P.M. shift till the end.

It was 4 A.M. Justin was having a frightening flashback. The medical staff tied his wrists so that he would not get up. He thought that the communist prison guards were tying him down. He threatened to sign himself out of the hospital unless they released him. He realized that I was with him and he thanked me for being his friend. Here I said something awful. "I would not be here if you had not kicked me out of the Philippines." He was crestfallen. Imagine being on your deathbed and having someone bring up issues of the past. At that moment God stepped in and corrected me in no uncertain terms. He said, "It was not Justin who sent you home. It was me. I called you home."

The time for Justin to rest was almost there. He had been almost dead about five times, but he kept reviving. I knew that at the time of a disciple's death Jesus came to bring him home. Now was the hour. I knew that Jesus was there in the room. All became still. At that moment Justin was moving on. It was 4:20 A.M.

I was asked to preach the eulogy. The funeral was held in the big church of Jamaica. I have often said that a funeral is only as great as the man in the box. The funeral was as big as Justin was great. **Justin was a great man of God.**

The other significant person in this story was Fr. Harold. He moved on to be a General Consultor in the Congregation in charge of watching over the Oceania area of the Pacific. He picked up a mystery virus and was on his way from Rome to the Leahy clinic in Massachusetts. This great international missionary began to die on the plane on the way home to America. He passed away a day after he got home. His funeral was great, too, but I failed to attend. I was on the road giving a mission. I was so sad I missed his Mass of Christian burial.

Fr. Ronan Callahan preached the eulogy. He did well in describing this very human being. I loved Harold like a brother. Here in Jamaica I visit his grave almost every day. Justin is buried about seven gravestones away. I pray to him, too. We were all brothers.

****

The story that I have told is true. It is my story. It is what it is. In some ways I wish I could delete all my mistakes and sins but then that would not be my story anymore. God had a "plan B" for me at every turn on the journey, but maybe it was all his "plan A". I invite you to ponder the mystery of your own story.

EPILOGUE

My life in the Spirit has been exciting. I have learned a lot of lessons. Some, the hard way. I'm sure there are many more lessons to learn. God wants us to be perfect. Whenever I would do something stupid, Yvonne would say, "Owen, you are too good not to be perfect." It was her gentle way of saying, "Shape up".

I pray always for a happy death. At first, I prayed to fall asleep some night and wake up in heaven. No feeding tubes, no needles, and no life supports. Nothing but my pajamas and me in my own bed. Then I looked at the ideal of my life, Jesus Crucified and my role as a Passionist. We are professional participators in the Redemption of the world. St. Paul the Apostle urges us "to bear our share of the hardship that the gospel entails".

"I rejoice, Lord, that I have been found worthy to suffer something for your name's sake". Have I done my share yet? I don't think so!

I conclude with the following prayer: "Lord, into your hands I commend my spirit. I accept whatever kind of death that you have for me. I TRUST IN YOUR MERCY! Thy will be done in me and through me.

Mary, my Mother, be with me now and at the hour of my death. Amen."

Acknowledgements

My mother, Irene was the great person in my life. There were many others, Yvonne Zeller, Harold Reusch, Justin Garvey, Peter Grace, and Ted Walsh.

Dr. Wilson Ko, M.D. Dr. Gregory Gustafson and Dr. Paul Lee, all of whom saved my life.

My Filipina co-workers, Sr. Ceferine Gordoncillo and Sr. Zenaida Matavia, and Sr. Carmen Franco. All my formators in the Paulacrucian charism, Frs. Ben Kelley, Mike Salvagna and the Word of the Cross Community.

In production and publishing, Fr. Victor Hoagland, Fr. Jack Douglas. Charles Vietrie, Fr. Thomas Anamattahil, Zeshan Bakht, Paul Zilonka, Rachel Gonzalez, Jean Alfano, Fr. Jim Ferry and the People of H.O.P.E. for getting me through the difficult days.

And finally
Dr. Herbert Gingold who saw that this was

A story that needed to be told

Appendix

"Job answered the Lord and said: I know that you can do all things and that no purpose of yours can be hindered. I have dealt with great things that I do not understand, things too wonderful for me, which I cannot know. I had heard of you by word of mouth but now my eye has seen you. Therefore I disown (the complaints I have said) and repent in dust and ashes.

The Lord restored the prosperity of Job and after he prayed for his friends: the Lord even gave him twice as much as he had before. Then all his brethren and sisters came to him and all his former acquaintances and they dined with him in his house. Thus the Lord blessed the latter days of Job more than his earlier ones. Then Job died, old and full of years."(Chapter 42)

Fr. Owen is now a member of the Passionist Senior Care Community in Jamaica, New York. He is still active in the Catholic Pentecostal Movement and hopes to celebrate the fiftieth anniversary of the Charismatic Renewal with Pope Francis in Rome in 2017.

If you would to order a hard copy of this book for you or a friend, you can do so via Amazon(.com)

Once on the site, enter "A Story That Needs To Be Told" or "Fr. Owen Lally" into the search bar and it will be the first result.

All proceeds will go towards the continuous funding of this project.

Thanks for all your support!

Made in the USA
San Bernardino, CA
28 March 2015